Dear Ann –
Happy belated Birthday
Thought This might interest
you as you'd met Mike
Actually ordered it in what
I Thought was Time for your
birthday.
  Ah well.. –
    Love
      Beth

The Lightbearer

*A True Story of Love, Death, and
Lessons Learned on the Other Side*

The Lightbearer

*A True Story of Love, Death, and
Lessons learned on the Other Side*

Bonnie Cox

Black Heron Press
Post Office Box 95676
Seattle, Washington 98145
www.blackheronpress.com

ISBN 0-930773-65-9

Black Heron Press
Post Office Box 95676
Seattle, Washington 98145
www.blackheronpress.com

I have loved two Michaels in my life.
I dedicate this book to both of them.

Acknowledgements

There are many people who have helped me to write and publish this book; friends and family members who gave me moral support, fellow writers and classmates who gave their editing support, and writing instructors who showed me the way. There are a few people to whom I'd like to give a special thank-you: Mike Sheerin, sky diver extraordinaire, who kept my technical descriptions on track; Nance Gruttman-Tyler, who helped me maintain my focus; Ib, for entrusting me with her son's memory; and Jeanne Poore-Jones-Zern-Wiley-Anderson for convincing me I could really do this and for helping me keep my sense of humor during the most difficult of times. I want to give my brother Jerry an extra-special thank-you for his editing and his belief in me. Most importantly, I'd like to thank my husband, Michael. He encouraged me to write openly about my love of Mike Jenkins. He's a shining example of how people can rise above personal insecurities to follow the guidance of their spirit.

Then in wonder I remembered the caressing,
stroking hands of the lightbearer.

— John Steinbeck

Prologue

Shortly after my twelfth birthday my spine began to curve sideways. At Children's Orthopedic Hospital in Los Angeles, treatments began with a body cast to control my errant spine and ended with two spinal fusions. There had been previous surgeries in my short life and more were to follow, but this experience remained unique.

It happened during the first spinal surgery. Under general anesthesia during past surgeries, time had ceased to exist. There was only the memory of going under and then, seemingly an instant later, waking up. But this time was different.

I was being released through myself, seeping through my own pores. My body could no longer contain me. The seeping gave way to a sensation of falling slowly through a tunnel. At first, I felt an impulse to grab on to something, to stop my fall. But this feeling was soon replaced with weightlessness as I began to rise, leaving my body on the operating table.

The lights overhead were no more than clouds I passed through, my attention now focused beyond the room, beyond the hospital. I looked out at the world as it passed beneath me. Briefly I regretted leaving my family and friends, but something inside me said it was time to let go.

Soon I felt as light as the atmosphere into which I was drawn, and I became united with everything that was around me, from the currents of the wind to the leaves of the trees that shimmered and swayed. Knowledge I didn't know I had now spoke to me as through an inner voice. My true existence had been put away, forgotten, but now I was re-experiencing it, unencumbered by a physical body, as though awakening from a deep sleep. The emotions and thoughts I had known were like a page that had just been turned as I passed on to a new chapter.

Soaring upward, I was fascinated and exhilarated by my flight. Below me I could see the earth's velvet blue curvature, but with infinite detail I could also see its people, animals, plants, and dwellings, as though I was looking through a zoom lens. There was a remarkable conduit of rippling energy, a thin, silver cord, connecting everything together. Through this umbilicus passed a moving, pulsing, stream of light to and from every person, animal, rock, and plant, down to the smallest blade of grass and into the earth itself. So connected, whatever affected one form of life affected all. This silver conduit spread before me like a web of rippling, breathing vibration.

As the earth fell away, I continued to remember,

like a recovering victim of amnesia, the structure of life's process. I saw my lives laid out as grains of sand on a beach, each grain representing a lifetime I had known or would know, one upon another, those past laying the foundation for the ones to come, yet all present together. I had shed my latest life and was once again spirit, dancing within a finer particle of existence. My spirit, along with all other life, had always been and always would be. I, like all life, was infinite.

Yet I saw that infinity has cycles, for my spiritual as well as physical life on earth. The experiences I'd had, shaped and refined the essence of my spirit. Each time I "died" my spirit emerged reshaped and redefined by the personality and events of that lifetime. Now I was going home, to my real home; to rest, to become restored, and someday to return again. For now, this was to be a time of processing, a time to appreciate more fully the addition to what was me.

With my recalled memory, I felt tremendous elation for I was returning to my father, not my biological father, but my real father, an all-knowing, all-loving, paternal energy, the source of all life, the creator and sculptor of all spirits. Awaiting me along with my father were numerous other energies, both male and female. As I approached them I could feel the radiance of their love, see the outline of their shapes in the atmosphere. Peace and tranquillity enveloped me like a soft cloak, fabricated from eons of shared journeys and the acceptance of our common spiritual bond. I was returning to my origin.

Abruptly, I awakened from surgery.

On the Other Side

1

My heart raced as I gulped the news. Fear consumed me, shutting down my mind. My hands lay limp and heavy on my lap, trembling. They seemed not to be mine. This isn't real — this can't be happening — a mistake! Everything will be fine. Kathy must be wrong — she misunderstood!

I rewound the memory tape in my mind, replaying the scene slowly, trying to find the flaw, a reason to disbelieve. I was sitting with Kathy in her nail salon when she picked up the phone. It was Dennis, her ex-husband.

"Oh my God," she said, "How?"

After a few monosyllables, she hung up and turned to me. "The Godflicker went in."

"What?" She couldn't have said "the Godflicker." It must be someone else. It couldn't be him, anyone on earth but him.

Kathy watched as I lost color. Then the pallor of recognition spread over her face. The man I had finally told her about only last week, the one I was in love with and had kept secret even from her, was Michael Jenkins, the Godflicker. Last week she had envied me. Now there was only pity in her eyes.

Kathy's ex-husband, like my own, was a skydiver. We had both divorced our husbands, but I had fallen in love with another jumper. I couldn't have lost him. I couldn't have. It just couldn't be.

"It was him, wasn't it?" Kathy wailed. "Oh my God, Bonnie, I'm so sorry. What can I do? Why didn't you tell me it was him? Oh my God! Why did I have to be the one to tell you?"

"There must be some mistake, Kathy..," I began.

"No," she shook her head, "there's no mistake! There were a dozen witnesses. He had a double malfunction over the lake and drowned. He cut away his main, but his reserve didn't fully open either. By the time they pulled him out of the water, it was too late. He was filming a jump..."

"...for *PM Magazine*." I finished. He had left my bed only this morning to do the shoot. This morning he was alive. I had touched his long, graceful body and kissed his sensuous lips only this morning.

Images from our last time together rushed to mind. There was something different about him this morning. When he stayed over, I usually left the house first. He liked to sleep in or relax and read for a while before leaving. But today I had had trouble with my car and he had offered to help. He usually encouraged me to be self-sufficient, but this morning he was especially attentive. He filled my battery with water, gave me a quick kiss through the open car window, turned to go, then came back to kiss me again.

Love has softened him, I thought. He's changing. Anyone who really knows him could see it. His
edginess was gone.

And now so was he.

The shop was suffocating. Patrons were staring
at us. I had to get out, go home. Maybe it had been a
mistake and he was waiting for me.

"Kathy, I have to go."

I grabbed my purse, but her hand clamped my
forearm. "You can't drive like this. Let me take you
home."

"No, I'll be okay, honestly. I need to go now!" I
rushed out the door and into my car before she could
stop me.

My mind insisted this couldn't be true. If Michael
had died, everything would stop. People wouldn't be
going about their business if he were really dead. If he
were gone from the earth, all other life would take
heed. Everything would be changed in some way. Look
out the window. Nobody's aware of any great change.
Therefore, Michael couldn't be dead.

I choked back the taste of bile in my throat,
barely controlling the nausea of fear. Calm down or
you'll never make it, I thought. You have to get home,
see for yourself. What if it was all a mistake and Michael
was there, waiting for me, but I was killed racing to get
home to him? I wanted to live in a world that held

Michael. Both of us alive or both dead. Either without
the other was unthinkable.

I screeched to a stop in my parking slot, tore the
key out of the ignition, and ran up the stairs to my
apartment. "Michael, Michael, are you there? Please be
there. Dear God, I'll give anything...!"

Coral — my cat — that time I thought she'd been
hit by a car — it was a case of mistaken identity. I'd seen
what looked like her body lying in the street and I'd
cried all the way home. Yet later that night her demand-
ing yowl had sounded at my door. I was so happy to see
her alive, I hugged her until she yelled. It was someone
else's cat that had died. Mine was still alive. Please,
dear God, let my Michael still be alive. I'm so sorry for
whoever died today, but please, don't let it be Michael.

The place was dark and still. I ran from room to
room, turning on lights, calling him, "Michael, please
be here, PLEASE!" But he was not.

The panic took hold now. I struggled to the
bedroom and saw his familiar signature: Our bathrobes
lay together on the bed, mine inside his, sleeves inter-
twined like arms around each other, collars against the
pillow — his reminder to me of how we are together
even when apart, safe in the folds of each other's love.

At that moment, I knew it was true. He was
gone. I fell into bed, burying my head in the robes, and
cried. I gasped for air, then began again, all the while
clinging to the soft fabric. The spicy scent of bath oil

still lingered in the fibers.

The sound of my telephone halted my sobs, but it couldn't be Michael calling, so I let it ring. The flashing red light on my answering machine told me of other calls today. In a moment I heard Earl's voice from the tinny speaker. He was one of Michael's closest friends.

"Bonnie, I have bad news," his voice broke. "I shouldn't leave this on your machine but I can't wait to talk to you in person." Then, more to himself, "I can't do this." Pause. "Michael is dead. It was a skydiving accident over Lake Elsinore today. I don't have all the details." Pause. "I hate doing this, but I promised, if it ever happened...I'm sorry this isn't in person. I just couldn't...I'm so sorry." Click. Dial tone.

Of course, other people's worlds have changed, too, like Earl's. There must be still others as well. "Who else?" I thought, as I reached over to rewind the tape and replay my messages.

My mother's voice spoke softly from the machine.

"Bonnie, if you're home, please pick up the phone. I need to talk to you." Pause...click...dial tone. Another message from my mother. "Bonnie, honey, please, if you're home, pick up the phone. I saw on the news that a photographer was killed over Lake Elsinore today. They didn't give his name. I hope to God it wasn't Michael. Please call me as soon as you can."

The news. Of course. Propelled by the promise of action, any action, I went into the living room, clutching the robes to my chest, and turned on the television. My body sank heavily onto the sofa, like a great, lifeless weight. I draped the robes over my lap and flipped the remote until I found a newscast. Finally I heard it.

"A freefall photographer was killed over Lake Elsinore today when his parachute failed to open. He was filming a segment for a television magazine program. His name is being withheld pending notification of his family." That was it. The news rolled on, other events affecting other people's lives, but no longer mine. I had my event for the day. It was the event of a lifetime.

"...family," the newscaster had said, reminding me of Ib, Michael's mother. Surely she knew by now. I had to call her. Let her know I knew.

Dialing, I could not imagine she would answer. She did.

"Ib, it's Bonnie."

"Hi." Her voice, hoarse and cracked, told me she knew.

"I'm so sorry." I began to cry.

"I know. Me, too," she sobbed.

Neither of us could speak. I finally managed, "I'll call you later when we can talk," and hung up.

In the bathroom I flipped on the light. It flickered several times before catching. I draped the robes over my shoulder and looked into the mirror. Swollen eyes stared back at me from a puffy face. The lights flickered again, dimmed, then brightened. I splashed cold water over my eyes, but the tears welled up again.

The signs of Michael's having been here were all around me: his hair brush beside the bathroom sink, breakfast dishes on the counter, a book on the coffee table. I walked through each room with leaden feet, noting the proof of his existence. He had walked here, touching these things, only a dozen hours ago. I did not wash or put anything away. I turned off the lights. It was nearly ten now. Exhausted, I didn't know if sleep would come, but I couldn't think of anything else to do. Bed seemed my only refuge.

Coral was suddenly bellowing at the front door. An outdoor cat, she liked a warm, safe place to sleep at night, usually at the foot of my bed. But when Michael stayed over, she shied from him and stayed under the bed. She wouldn't share my bed with him in it. She had challenged Michael's ability to win favor with animals. He couldn't woo her, but he respected her feelings. Now my heart lifted at her sound. She was my miracle cat who had survived when I'd thought her dead. I went quickly to the front door and turned on the hall light.

"Come in, Coral, it's time for bed."

She paused at the threshold, startled, her slightly crossed eyes staring at a point just over my left shoulder. I felt a tingling along my shoulder and neck, the area of her gaze, and turned quickly to see what was there. Nothing. When I turned back, she was gone. I called her name, but she was invisible in the night. She wouldn't come to me. Finally I closed the door. I would have liked to have her soft body curling against my feet, her purring lulling me to sleep. Why wouldn't she come in?

I went into the bathroom to brush my teeth. The lights flickered again, then settled into a more diffuse illumination, reminding me of the candles Michael and I had burned as we bathed together. Contented by the embrace of the scented water, we would watch the light of the flames bounce unevenly off the tile. I could almost hear yesterday's stereo music filter through the walls from the living room.

Suddenly the light went out completely, leaving me in darkness. It seemed appropriate that today, these lights, like his life, would be extinguished.

I stumbled to bed, my way lighted by the bedside lamp. My anguish again filled the room. Eyes shut tight, I cried aloud, "Michael, take me with you. I can't stand it here without you. Wherever you are, let me be with you."

My eyes opened and I gasped. He was here, his face and upper torso suspended in the air just above me. His pained expression showed he understood the enormity of what had happened to him. I reached out to

all we would ever need. I continued to marvel at his existence, aware even in this "dream" that he was supposed to be dead. I had never had a dream so vivid and alive in detail. He called it "the other side," a term that seemed familiar.

2

Morning came reluctantly. The sense of peace and love from the other side lingered as I began to awaken. I stretched, savoring the feelings and images, remembering as much as I could. A feeling of privilege remained, of having visited a sacred place. I'd seen a land whose presence I couldn't explain and to which travel was beyond my comprehension, yet I felt awakened to something, something recalled from a memory beyond memory.

I considered the possibilities. At best, Michael now existed on another side of reality and I had somehow been able to visit it last night. At worst, the shock of his death had driven me insane and this was some elaborate hallucination. All that I had experienced last night might be nothing more than a wishful dream. If I were really mad though, would I have the presence of mind to question myself?

Or maybe it was something else. Perhaps he was somewhere else and was able to communicate with me in a way I didn't understand. I'd had a few clairvoyant experiences in the past, usually at the most unguarded moments. When my grandmother died I saw her face in a flash of light superimposed on my father's face at what turned out to be the exact time of her death, three hours before the family was to learn of it.

On another occasion, I was driving my old Renault when I saw flames encircling me. The vision had scared me so badly that I borrowed money from my father to buy a new car. I later learned that the person who had bought the Renault from me had been involved in a fatal auto accident in that car. I always felt guilty after that for selling the car at all. I should have had the courage of my intuition and just sold it for junk or had it destroyed. It had not occurred to me that the vision of being engulfed in flames might not have been meant to apply to me, but to someone else, or perhaps to the car itself.

It was difficult to connect reason with these kinds of phenomena. Where did these visions come from, and why? The prediction of the car at least had saved my life, but for what purpose? Why had I been spared and not the subsequent car owner? I had no answers. Now the experience of last night posed other questions. As the dream continued to fade, the only certainty I had was the memory of Michael's death yesterday. I tried to fathom the impact that losing him would have on the rest of my life but my mind wouldn't focus on anything but my immediate loss.

I couldn't just continue to lie in bed and go into another crying fit. Action was needed to temper my grief. I remembered the burned-out light in the bathroom and forced myself out of bed to call the apartment manager. A handyman showed up within twenty minutes with two boxed, six-foot-long fluorescent bulbs. He was alone in the bathroom for only a few moments when I heard him say, "Well, I'll be damned."

"What's the matter?" I asked, going into the bathroom.

"You don't need new bulbs here. Somehow both these bulbs got twisted out of their sockets. But I'll be damned if I know how. 'Specially two of them. We didn't have an earthquake last night, I know of. Don't know how that could've done this anyway. Well, I popped yours back in. Now they got juice again, they're good as new." He flipped the light switch on and off, proving how well they worked. We both looked from the light above to the unused bulbs. He picked them up and left.

As I left the bathroom, I looked up at the lights that were, then weren't, then were again. "Was that you, Michael?"

In the kitchen, I stood waiting for a tea bag to steep in a cup of hot water as I wondered what to do next. Ib and Tom, Michael's stepfather, would be planning his funeral, sorting through his personal effects, attending to the details of his burial. Perhaps they could use my help, but I felt like an accident victim myself. I was suffering an inertia that rendered me incapable of anything but the most rudimentary action. There was a feeling of urgency to do something, but the only thing I longed to do was to go back in time and reverse yesterday's events.

My eyes wandered to the corner of the dining room where I had set up my art studio. What had started as a semi-serious pastime had become part of my livelihood. My painting gave me the creative outlet I craved and my work had become popular, at first with friends, then, by word of mouth, with others who commissioned me to paint particular pieces.

My current painting, however, had moved me to put my commission work aside. I had come across an anonymous snapshot six weeks earlier that had inspired me to translate it to canvas. A single moment of joy was caught in a photo of a boy and girl, five or six years old, as they ran with abandon. Complete happiness showed on their faces. Their pink skin framed by deep, rich hues of greenery captured the lushness of nature and the natural exuberance of youth. When I first saw the photograph, I thought how precious moments like these were, and I was drawn to capture the emotion of these unknown children so that I could remember the existence of that pure joy. I needed to remember it all the more now.

I picked up a paint brush, added color to the bristles, and began to lose myself in the canvas. The underpainting was complete. It was time to go over it again, deepening the hues with more color, cooling and darkening the shadowed areas, highlighting and warming each part touched by the sun. It reminded me of the light and happiness on the other side, and also of how Michael and I became close. Ironically, I had my ex-husband to thank for that. My mind settled into the serenity of the scene. As I touched each child, each leaf, with pigment, I became part of the picture, releasing my grief and pain, remembering the beginning.

It was Larry's smoky smile that first attracted me to him. His dark Italian coloring, wavy black hair, and down-turned eyes reminded me of Dean Martin. Like the actor, he had a self-effacing charm and charisma that endeared him to people. It wasn't until after we were married that I realized his charm was simply his attempt to compensate for a forbidding melancholy. Early disappointments and a harsh upbringing had taught him to expect little of life. His favorite homily was, "If I didn't have bad luck, I wouldn't have no luck at all." I loved him though and wanted to be a shining ray of hope to counter his often dark disposition.

He had been going alone to Lake Elsinore's skydiving center every weekend for months. I viewed skydiving as a frivolous and extravagant death wish disguised as a sport. How could the adrenaline rush of jumping out of an airplane at 12,000 feet be worth the risk of death? I had had too many broken bones, surgeries, and near disasters to court more danger.

At first I ignored his new interest, thinking that if I didn't support it, he would eventually choose spending time with me over skydiving. As it turned out, I was to be more transient in his life than the sport. He was becoming obsessive about it. Everything else was beginning to take a back seat, including me. I realized then that I needed to either join him or risk losing him.

My first introduction to some of the skydivers was at a pizza party. It was one of the few times jumpers got together away from the drop zone. My goal was simple: save my marriage by finding a way to become a part of my husband's new interest.

At the party, a free-fall photographer named Michael Jenkins, otherwise known as "the Godflicker," showed motion pictures of his craft: the filming of skydivers in freefall. He earned his name by becoming the photographer, or flicker, of "sky gods," those talented jumpers distinguished from others by their greater dedication and ability.

The first sequence of shots showed an exit from the open door of a DC3. He must have gone first, on his back, with the others jumping out nearly on top of him and each other. They hurtled themselves from the airplane in their brightly colored jumpsuits with expressions of jubilant expectancy.

From the first few frames the jumpers in the restaurant whooped and hollered, adding audio counterpoint to the moving pictures as they relived their experience. In the next sequence, Michael floated above them. He had fitted his jumpsuit with wings, triangular fabric insets sewn from hips to wrists on either side, that he could flare and slow his fall, as he wished. Although first out of the plane, he could turn his belly to earth and spread his wings, catching more air than the other jumpers in order to float above them, apart from them, yet connected to them through his lens.

I was entranced. As I looked around the darkened room I saw the jumpers totally immersed in the scenes on the screen, as if they didn't know how the story would end.

In the film, two men started the formation of a circle, called a "star," by connecting to each other. They held onto the wrists of each other's jumpsuits and became the base and pin for others to join. As more jumpers flew to them, the circle quickly expanded. Each new jumper joining the circle would grip the wrists of the two jumpers on either side of where he wanted to enter. He would then secure his grip on each adjoining jumpsuit by twisting the fabric, making a larger handle to hold. When his doubled-gripped hold was accomplished he would shake the wrists of the jumpers on either side as a signal that they could release from each other, making him a part of the whole.

Twenty jumpers, men and women, flew from all directions to join the circle, all the while falling hundreds of feet per second. The goal was to get them all into the formation before they ran out of time, out of sky. They looked as if they were flying, not falling. Michael circled the group like a satellite in orbit around planetary bodies. The jumpers' heads, cocooned in helmets of plastic or leather, lifted as they looked into each other's faces with huge grins below amber goggles.

As each jumper found a slot and carved his way into the circle, the jumpers in the room added their commentary. "Smokin', Kelley!" at a jumper who bombed his way to the star a little too fast but slowed just in time to avoid crashing the formation. A few seconds later I heard, "Has to be Reardon," referring to a more timid jumper who kept trying to lower himself into the star but each time flared too soon and rose above it. Then whoops and laughter at the Hand Walker, a jumper who grabbed not the wrists of each jumper but their arms, and inched his way down their sleeves until he found a handhold he trusted. Another jumper overshot his mark and rather than hit the star, somersaulted over it, making a swan dive through the middle. "Bye bye, Hansen," someone mocked. But there was also a moment of respectful acknowledgments of, "Yeh," "All right," at Hansen, who sacrificed his own position in the star to avoid taking out the rest.

The jumpers were now connected. In the room, they yelled like a football team at a hard-earned touchdown. On the screen, they were laughing, their joy undisguised. Their arched torsos and bent legs rode the waves of the wind like seagulls drifting in a breeze. Spellbound, the film drew me to them, inviting me in. I felt the thrill of their flight and saw their exhilaration. They were one with the ultimate freedom — space — and with each other. In their moment of completion, these men and women who had come together, irrespective of age, profession, or social status, had formed a union of spirit that bound them to one another far more than the handholds that connected their circle.

Their joy cleared my vision. I saw then that skydiving was different from the dangers I had known in my own life. There had been nothing joyous about scores of surgeries and accidents. Those were beyond my control. For the jumpers, skydiving was the chance to extend themselves to their fullest abilities, knowing that failure could mean death, but having the courage to do it anyway. It was a combination of the best life had to offer coupled with fear of the worst. They weren't waiting for life to test them. They were doing it themselves.

Larry worked for a plumbing contractor and I worked for a doctor in Orange County. Our jobs were okay, but by Wednesday of each week, we began to look forward to the weekend at Elsinore. It was the weekends that made the rest worthwhile. Jumping offered the excitement in life that had been denied Larry in his youth. The oldest of four sons, he became a father and husband before he was out of his teens and was forced into a level of familial responsibility far beyond what he was ready for. Drive-in movies and carhop burgers were for young men who had the luxury of free time and extra spending money. Larry had had neither.

Elsinore accorded me the camaraderie of people I respected and admired. Much of my youth had been spent without close friendships due to an assortment of health problems. From mononucleosis to heart surgery, the breakdown of my body seemed to be interspersed only with short intervals of being well and active. Spending time with a sick friend was never a high priority for most of my classmates. Larry, with his own frailties, gave me little more attention than I'd received from my school friends. Jumpers, however, became our friends and then became our extended family. For the first time, I was an accepted part of a group I had come to love. I carved a niche for myself as someone who supported the sport and appreciated the participants.

The skydiving center was located a few miles south of the lake. The town lay mostly on the lake's northeastern border, cradled in a valley surrounded by low hills. Its permanent residents were mostly retirees on fixed pensions attracted to the inexpensive desert housing. On the first of each month, when the social security checks arrived, lines of elderly crowded the banks. They liked to cash their Medicare checks for greenbacks that they carried on them for the day. It made them feel rich. But by the second day of the month, practicality ruled as they again filed into the banks to deposit the cash into their checking accounts to pay their bills.

The area was high desert. It offered mostly dry, hot temperatures in the summer, and freezing cold winds, sometimes laced with snow, in the winter. The stark terrain of brown earth, sage, cactus, and scrub oak could be transformed into a luxurious emerald-green carpet overnight by just one rainfall. But that was rare. Mostly, the desert remained unadorned, like a natural beauty without make-up. Riotous, flowering color erupts more easily in other, lusher climates. But the desert draws attention through her unpredictable moods — sudden outbursts of lightning and thunder are easily forgiven when followed by backlit clouds of brilliant silver festooned with triple rainbows.

Our weekend home became a fifteen-foot-long trailer parked permanently alongside other mobile relics from a long-past decade. I awakened Saturday and Sunday mornings to the sound of the jump planes warming up and taking off, a hundred yards from my pillow.

The sport beckoned to me as well. I rose above my fear of physical injury and completed the theory section of the First Jump Course. But when I jumped off the six-foot platform in full gear for practice landings,

I couldn't get up. My spine had been fused when I was thirteen and most of its function as a natural shock absorber had been eliminated. My career as a skydiver would be extremely limited without the ability to land safely.

I complained of this to Dirty Ed. A Skygod of immeasurable talent and dedication, he was skydiving's equivalent of a surf bum. He worked at jobs only so he could afford to jump. We sat on a bench outside the manifest office, where jumps and lessons were scheduled and flights were announced on the loudspeaker.

"I want to be a jumper, Ed but my spine is fused. I'm afraid of breaking it on a landing."

I expected him to reply with, Oh, you'll be fine. You'll learn to compensate. The experience will be worth it.

He looked at me with what was, for him, a soft expression and rubbed his own back. "I wrecked my back, too. Jumping has cost me a lot." Looking off at the sky, then back at me, he said, "I'm not saying it wasn't worth it, but you'd be crazy to do it."

I bent my head as if I'd heard the final verdict. I was both disappointed and relieved.

My participation in the sport was to be as ground assistant for the women's sky diving team, "Madame Sally and the Sky Hookers." The team name was a parody on the men's championship skydiving team,

"Captain Hook and the Sky Pirates," whose captain wore a hook to replace the hand he had lost in Viet Nam.

I accompanied the women to demonstration jumps at the Dinah Shore Golf Classic, the Can Am car races at Riverside, and shopping mall openings. I did the announcing on the microphone. Women athletes who excelled in macho sports were a novelty that advertising promoters loved.

At Elsinore, I organized the women between jumps and entered them on the manifest. I made sure they took time to eat and had enough liquids to drink during the day. They couldn't afford the filming services of the Godflicker, so I watched their jumps through binoculars, timing their exits and star formations with a stop watch. Besides keeping in shape for the demo jumps, they practiced year around for the national and international championships held each year.

The few times I saw the Godflicker around the drop zone after the pizza party, he both frightened and thrilled me. His tanned skin, dark eyes, black hair, and trimmed mustache and Van Dyke beard reminded me of photographs from a past era, or in especially imaginative moments, heroes from gothic romance novels. His six-feet-two-inch frame sported limbs disproportionately long for his torso and would have seemed gangly but for the easy grace with which he moved. He walked with a quiet gate that was propelled from the balls of his feet, never coming fully to rest on his heels.

Although I'd never talked to him, he emitted an energy and intensity that drew me to him, yet intuitively warned me that he was a man who could get too close, see too much. I saw in his eyes something that would tolerate only truth and I was living in a tenuous marriage, pretending to be happy and fulfilled.

I had hoped that through the shared love of skydiving and its participants Larry and I would become closer. Instead, we drifted further apart. We both got from Elsinore what we wanted, but it didn't seem to be each other. I could only describe our marriage as a light varnish of affection coating an increasing lack of intimacy. Yet I was not ready to give up. It could be dangerous if I allowed another man to fill the void between Larry and me. Perhaps it would be safe to become friends with Michael, but I was still a married woman who was unwilling to shake the cobwebs from my love life.

Because of Larry, I was introduced to Lake Elsinore and skydiving. Because of my huge, lumbering St. Bernard, Brandy, I was introduced to Michael. Brandy decided one afternoon that the wooden bench on which Michael was lying was close enough to being a tree that he could leave his mark on it. A tall dog, he missed the side of the bench, making a direct hit on Michael's thigh. My embarrassment immediately

turned to nervous laughter. Every time I tried to apolo-
gize, some abominable noise — a snort, a gasp, a wheeze
— rose from my throat. Finally, I managed to cough
out, "I'm so sorry..."

Of all the people for Brandy to "piss off," why
did it have to be him? Besides the fact that I found him
intimidating, he had a reputation for biting wit mixed
with his own brand of sarcastic humor: his retort would
come and all you could do was get out of the way.

I waited for his zinger, still immobile from laughter. Perhaps he took pity on me or simply couldn't be
angry with a woman in the throes of convulsive, stac-
cato giggles. The corners of his lips barely edged up as
he replied, "It's been that kind of a day." He rose
without attempting to wipe himself off, and slowly
strolled away.

Over the following months, Michael and I became more aware of each other. Our paths had rarely
crossed around the drop zone before the Brandy inci-
dent. Now we exchanged glances, smiles, and remarks
several times a day. "Do you have any other pets you'd
like me to potty train?" he whispered once in passing.

One afternoon I was holding tension lines for
Sally as she was repacking her rig. The canopy top was
hooked to a peg in the ground with the suspension lines
extending from the parachute canopy to the housing
pack attached to them. I "sat" in the pack, my weight
creating a tension on the lines, enabling Sally to

straighten and untangle them for the repack.

It must have been over a hundred degrees that day, a hot day portending an even hotter summer. Most of us had learned to adapt to the heat by drinking lots of water, conserving energy whenever possible, and wearing little clothing. I was wearing standard Elsinore attire: a halter top, shorts, visor, and lots of suntan lotion.

Occasionally, some women and a few men took advantage of the weather conditions to cater to their exhibitionist tendencies. Walking alongside the grassy packing area that afternoon was the girl friend of one of the Sky Gods. She had brought her *Playboy* layout to the drop zone, showing her "spread" to any of the men who wished to see her au naturel. On this day, however, she needn't have bothered. Her attire was a tiny triangle over each nipple, suspended from her neck and tied at her back by a string that could have been spun by a pygmy spider. The bottom half was little more than a G string. I was frankly admiring the rehearsed nonchalance of her walk, as if she didn't notice the men around her tripping over their tension lines or pouring water over their hot bodies instead of into them.

Michael appeared beside me. "There are two kinds of women who frequent the drop zone," he said. "Those who come to hold tension and those who come to create it."

We both looked at the living centerfold and

laughed.

Then, looking straight at me, he continued, "There are, of course, exceptions — those who do both."

Lunch

3

My marriage had been declining, like land slowly eroding, hillock by hillock. With each bit lost, I viewed what remained and thought, Well there's enough left, I can live with that. But suddenly the erosion became an avalanche. Everything in my life changed, even the way in which I viewed myself, when I found a lump in my left breast.

On first examining me, my doctor thought I had a fast-growing cyst in the breast's inner, lower quadrant. When he operated soon after, he found that the prosthetic implant under my breast had ruptured and infiltrated two-thirds of my breast, gone into my sternum and seeped into the surrounding flesh. The surgery consisted of blotting out as much of the gooey mess as possible and cutting out the affected tissue and skin.

Because he was afraid that I would sue him for disfiguring me, the doctor did not tell me what he'd done. The padded surgical dressing and his silence hid the truth from me for the first week following surgery. When I came to his office to have the dressing changed, he left the room just before his nurse gave me a mirror to see my body for myself.

I don't remember screaming, or hyperventilating, or shaking, or crying, but I must have done it all. I do remember other nurses coming into the room with a paper bag to put over my mouth and nose, a blanket for shock, and smelling salts.

Larry was waiting in the car. When I finally joined him there almost an hour later, he saw my drawn face. "What's the matter? Why did it take so long?"

I whispered hoarsely, "He cut off my breast...most of it...the left one."

"You mean he took out the implants?"

"That, too. One broke...it infiltrated...the breast is gone."

I waited for something, some sign from Larry that my entire life had not just changed. Something that would put what had just happened into a different perspective. I wanted him to hold me, to tell me everything was going to be all right.

His face contorted in anger. "It's your own fault!" he yelled. "I told you not to have that damned surgery. Now look what you've done!"

In my head I answered him because my voice could not: You told me a thousand times how much you wanted me to have this surgery by your sidelong looks every time you passed a large-breasted woman. You told me a hundred times what a great figure I had, except I could use a little help "up front." You told me after the surgery how, now, I was perfect. You told me everything except what I needed to hear: I love you just as you are.

In 1976, flower children were still commonplace, love was free and easy, and inflation was eating away at people's savings. When the economy went into a recession it caused a slowdown in the building industry and Larry lost his job. It didn't take him long to decide that what he really wanted to do for a living was what he loved best: skydiving. The sport could become his livelihood if he became an instructor. There was little money in it but we had both come to love Lake Elsinore and we decided to make it our new home.

Elsinore proved to be, for me, the haven I had hoped for: a tranquil world filled with people who shared a common bond. Unlike life in the city, living in Elsinore was laid back and slow-paced. We took the equity from the sale of our house in Orange County and bought a double-wide mobile home, planting it on ten acres of land in Wildomar, five miles from the skydiving center.

Our new home, surrounded by ranches and open terrain, perched atop the highest hill in the area from which we had a 360-degree view of rolling pasture land peppered with hay bales, wooden barns, and acres of wheat, oats, and alfalfa. Ancient California oaks stood silhouetted like gnarled sentinels. Beyond lay the Ortega Mountains that cut through the Cleveland National

Forest. In the stillness I could hear the nickering of
horses and, at night, the synchronized howling of coy-
otes. It would have been idyllic there with the right
man. The lifestyle and pastoral environment was a
balm to my shattered self-image, but all the long dying
of my marriage undercut my contentment.

The bread and butter of Michael's career was
filming the competition teams, an often exhausting and
sometimes dangerous job. In freefall, he had to be in the
best possible position for filming the star while staying
out of the way of the other bodies falling around him.
He played the film for the jumpers between jumps,
enabling them to critique their performance. Since a
dedicated competition team could jump five to seven
times a day, Michael spent a great deal of time in the air.
But now, between jumps and film reviews, he was
around a lot more.

I couldn't understand his interest in me. After
all, I was unavailable, and he had never seemed to lack
for female companionship. He had a reputation for
appreciating women and judging by the looks they
gave him, the feeling was mutual.

Michael loved to study human nature and I was
learning from him. He often amazed me by his predic-
tions of the outcome of his fellow jumpers' relationships, based on his observations of their personalities,
what they communicated through their speech, and,

more importantly, by their facial expressions and body language. This was not intended for entertainment but, rather, stemmed from his compassion for his "pa'dners."

One hot afternoon between jumps Michael sat beside me on the grass, reclining on an elbow. As he looked off at the Ortegas, he seemed to be considering his words before speaking. An alarm sounded in me. I had seen that same contemplative look just before he had spoken of others' difficult situations. Now he was aiming his sights at me. I had a feeling he was about to confront me with something I wasn't ready to face.

The gulf between Larry and me had continued to widen and now I suspected that he was having an affair. My entire life had changed with the restructuring of my body, and I felt even more demeaned as a woman and discarded as a wife. But I had done nothing about it. The wreck of my life had left debris scattered all around, yet I had looked the other way for so long, I'd gotten used to living in ruins.

"Have you ever felt cherished?" Michael asked softly. His choice of words cut deep. Larry had dedicated the song "Cherish" to me nine years earlier when we became engaged and our relationship seemed full of promise. If Michael asked the question, he must already know the answer.

"I thought I was cherished, once," I answered. I grabbed my sunglasses to hide my tears and excused myself.

My unhappiness finally surfaced in a way I couldn't ignore when a few days later, one of the women's team members stopped by for tea. Over a cup of Constant Comment, she simply asked, "How are you?"

I burst into tears, looking only at the tablecloth in front of me. "I'm so miserable. I feel so deserted. My marriage is virtually gone and I don't know how to get it back!"

Shocked at my own outburst, I stopped and looked at her. Her face was scarlet, her eyes wide with disbelief. Her hand and teacup were frozen halfway to her mouth.

In suspended time, we faced each other in horror, like two women who've just been told that one of them has an incurable disease, without being told which one. I fought to regain control of myself and changed the subject, realizing too late that she'd be appalled at being caught in a conflict between Larry and me. We tried to make light conversation for awhile but then, before the steam had left her cup, she remembered someplace else she had to go.

Pretense was useless now. There was nowhere to look but at my pain. If Larry was being unfaithful, I had to know. If disappointment and discontent had not been enough to end my marriage, infidelity would. I could not continue to live in this chaos.

That evening, before Larry could retreat to the

television after dinner, I gathered my courage and looked him in the face. "Are you having an affair?"

"What are you talking about? No, no, of course not," he stammered, avoiding my eyes. "I'd never do anything to jeopardize our marriage. You know that." But his tone sounded condescending rather than reassuring.

"Jeopardize our marriage," he'd said. Not "I'd never do anything to hurt you." The distinction was not lost on me. I felt that if he thought he could keep me from discovering his affair, he would be reasonably certain I wouldn't end the marriage and he need not suffer the guilt of divorcing his maimed wife.

But his withdrawal from me had already hurt deeply. Since my mastectomy, our bed was the only thing we shared and it was no longer used for anything but sleep.

It was time to confess my misery to Kathy. If I could confide in anybody, it would be her. She'd had her own experience with infidelity, once confronting her husband when he returned home wearing his undershorts inside out. She was in her element when I asked for help.

"What you need to do," she directed, "is keep track of his whereabouts and look for patterns of absence that are out of character. And look over your phone bill for calls to numbers you don't recognize.

You'll be amazed at the trail they leave."

I found such a pattern on Tuesdays, and a number of long distance calls to a number in San Diego. The telephone company provided me with the name of the person. She was a student jumper named Sandra. This looked suspicious, of course, but it wasn't proof.

As I sat in the shade at the drop zone one afternoon, Larry walked out of the manifest office into the brilliant sunlight. He didn't see me sitting at the packing table. As he strolled in front of me, his face lit up with a soft look I hadn't seen in years. But his gaze wasn't for me. Approaching him from the opposite direction was Sandra. Their eyes met and their smiles revealed two people in love, or at least in lust. Had I been sitting a couple of inches to one side or the other, I'd never have seen both their faces at once. No matter what Larry said now, I knew he was involved with her.

Dazed and shaken, I found a quiet spot under a shade tree to be alone for awhile. I stretched out on my side, cradling my head in the crook of my arm and studied the tree bark, knowing that very soon I would have to make decisions about the rest of my life. I had sought the truth and had found it in a way I could neither mistake nor ignore. But for the moment, I wanted only to study the tree. A column of large, black ants wound their way up the bark. Their circuitous route took them around shingles of various sizes. If a protrusion was too high to scale, they went around it, always moving upward. In my mopishness I wondered if ants always knew where they were going, regardless of the obstacles.

"You look like you could use a friend," Michael offered as he sat down beside me. The sunlight filtered through the tree's leaves and fell on the grass beside us, dappling the ground with alternating hues of green. My eyes noted this contrast before I looked up and saw the compassion in his eyes.

"How right you are." My voice sounded frail and distant. I did not want to be alone anymore. I sat up.

He plucked a blade of grass, began to chew on it and said, "Come on, let me feed you and we'll talk."

There were a few cafes and restaurants in the area but the casino had the best food in town. It was as elegant as Elsinore got. Over Monte Cristo sandwiches we talked about marriage and relationships in general. Then we talked about mine. I started from the beginning, how I had always felt the necessity to try to make my marriage work, no matter what the circumstances. To me, marriage should be bigger than the individuals involved.

Michael listened without interruption as I confided in him. "You know," I said, "it's ironic. So many people have said that, in this day and age of revolving relationships, our marriage is an inspiration to them. I feel that on some level we would be letting them down by divorcing."

"Maybe," he said, "they have little else to inspire them." He paused, musing over a french fry, then continued. "People tend to see what they choose. You don't have to answer me, but ask yourself: Of the eight or nine years you and Larry have been married, how many have been happy?"

I did not answer. I could not recall one completely happy year.

"The only real obligation you have in this life is to be the best Bonnie you can be. No matter what form that takes or who else is in your life, the main commitment and responsibility you have is to yourself, who you are, who you become. That, in fact, is all you have any control over."

I began to see myself from the outside. The thought both thrilled and scared me. I had a lot of work to do to discover who I was without being paired with a man. Yet I knew that I did not want to face the rest of my life alone.

"What if no one ever loves me again?" I asked, whispering the words for fear of giving them power.

He smiled. "Why would you even think that possible? Do you believe you are so unlovable?"

"I've had a partial mastectomy," I said softly.

"I know," he said, matter-of-factly, and popped a pickle chip into his mouth.

"How do you know?"

"There are no secrets around the drop zone, Bonnie. There's only Do-you-know-it-now-or-later? Why does the mastectomy bother you so much?"

I couldn't believe he'd asked this question. Surely he must realize that most women feel that their breasts symbolize their sexuality. To lose my sexual attractiveness at thirty was devastating. Perhaps he'd asked to test my reaction.

"I'm disfigured and there's nothing plastic surgery can do for me."

"Disfigured like this?" he asked, holding up his left pinkie finger, revealing that half of it was missing. "A skydiving accident."

"Yes, like that" I said. We both smiled, then laughed. I went on. "I can't imagine being attractive to a man, looking the way I do. I can't imagine a man not being repulsed by my breast. Larry evidently was."

"Bonnie, a man responds to a woman sexually based on how she feels about herself and how she feels about the man. That has nothing to do with how she looks compared to a centerfold. She could be truly unattractive or have no breasts at all, but she could turn on a man far more than a beautiful woman who believes herself ugly. Sexuality flows from here," he said, tapping the top of my head.

Perhaps he really believed that, but it didn't change how I felt. I'd wanted Larry to see me as unblemished so that, through him, I could see myself the same way. It hadn't worked. The vision of Larry and Sandra played again in my mind.

We'd come this far, so I asked, "Is Larry having an affair?" Even though I knew the answer, I didn't want the humiliation of everyone else knowing. Considering the number of jumpers Michael came in contact with, I figured he would be the most accurate barometer of what was known around the drop zone.

"Yes. But you knew that or you wouldn't have asked. Why do you think I asked you about being cherished?"

"I guess I knew. But I'm not prepared for it to be common knowledge."

"I don't think it's common knowledge. But if you're worried about what the jumpers would think of you because your old man is playing around, they'd probably think pretty much as I do."

"What's that?"

"That Larry is one of the greatest fools in Elsinore, and there are already enough of those. To give up a Bonnie for a Sandra is incomprehensible."

"Thank you." I replied, tears of gratitude filling my eyes. "Thank you for being my friend and for being honest about Larry."

"Honesty is cheap in the long run. It's lying that's expensive. Especially when it's to yourself. A winner walks away, Bonnie. A loser stays and takes it. You're neither burned out nor dried up. I've seen plenty of people like that. They're the ones who come into my folks' liquor store day after day to buy a pint at a time. The light still glows in your eyes, Bonnie. Do something for yourself while you can."

He was right. My depression was caused less by the breakup of my marriage than by my refusal to do something about it. For some time I had been denying the agony in which I was living. The truth was that despite our initial attraction, Larry and I were not compatible. I had always craved closeness through communication, but this was very difficult for Larry. Getting him to disclose his private thoughts and feelings was like trying to pry open a walnut with a toothpick. Early in our relationship I had been able to wheedle his thoughts from him only after an eternity of coaxing. But that had become increasingly difficult and eventually impossible. I suppose reticence is a characteristic many people share. I just wasn't one of them, and should never have married someone who was.

In addition, it had been my parents and not he who had seen me through the ordeals of heart surgeries, back surgeries and illnesses. A couple of years after we married, I returned home from work early, racked by a 104-degree fever accompanied by chills and chattering teeth. He came home after work, saw my physical state and asked, "Aren't you fixing dinner?"

No, his infidelity was not the only reason to end our marriage; it was just the latest.

I felt ashamed for not having had the courage to call it quits before. Had I let myself get beaten down because I thought I had no options? Michael had not told me anything I didn't already know, but his words were a butt-kicking inspiration aimed at launching me into action.

As though he were reading my mind, he said, "To quote a really wise man: 'How well you bear the mark of where you've been is the proof of who you'll be.'"

"Who said that?" I asked.

"I did," he said, grinning like the Cheshire cat.

I laughed.

He touched my forearm with his half-finger and said, "You have nothing to be afraid of."

All right, I was leaving Larry. But when? Tomorrow was our eighth wedding anniversary. It would be too callous to end things on the eve of our anniversary. Our friend, Sid, was taking us out for dinner in Beverly Hills and had gotten us tickets to "A Chorus Line." Somehow I would get through tomorrow night. Then I would find a way.

Sid had made arrangements for us to meet him at his Los Angeles condo at 6:00. He'd given Larry a key to his place in case we got there before him. Larry and I both knew by the Mercedes, thousand-dollar watches and designer clothes that Sid, a businessman who owned

a chain of jewelry stores, was rich. But neither of us
fully appreciated his wealth until we let ourselves into
his home. It was exquisitely furnished in expensive,
contemporary bachelorhood: black Spanish leather so-
fas and chairs, plush white carpet, chrome and beveled-
glass tables accented with abstract marble and bronze
statuary. Lithographs and oil paintings hung on the
walls. With the press of a button, a state-of-the-art
lighting system, music system, and entertainment center sprang to life.

My first thought was, This place is so immacu-
late, he must have a maid. Larry spoke his first reaction
aloud: "My God, to be single and live like this! What
a life!"

To hell with anniversaries, I thought. This marriage should have ended yesterday.

I don't remember what I ate or at what restaurant. The play was advertised as a hit but I wouldn't
know. My eyes were open but unseeing. Larry's on the
other hand weren't even open. He slept through the
play. Sid was a good sport but could see the obvious.
This was not the interaction of two happily married
people. He had meant the evening to be a thank-you for
our friendship and had gone to a great deal of trouble
to make it memorable. He would never know just how
memorable it was.

The next morning, I emerged dressed from our
bedroom and found Larry on the living room sofa

breathing evenly with his eyes closed. He'd slept there all night but this morning I believed he was just playing possum.

"Our marriage is over," I told him. My voice was detached, quiet, but firm. He opened his eyes without looking at me and said nothing in reply. Then he turned his face away and closed his eyes again.

That afternoon I moved in with a girl friend in Elsinore until I could find my own place and devise a plan of action for my future. I may have left Larry in haste, but there were no more excuses for staying.

I called Michael as soon as I could. "I've left him."

"You have," he said, more as a statement than a question. "How do you feel?"

"Relieved, happy, sad, scared, proud. All of the above. But above all, I know I've made the right decision. It's just that, I guess there's a mourning period when a marriage ends."

"Well, just be careful where your grief takes you," he warned.

"What do you mean?"

Avoiding my question, he asked his own, "Where will you be staying?"

Could this be an invitation? I couldn't stay with him even if he were to ask me. If I went directly from Larry to Michael, everyone would think I'd left one for the other. It would be a convenient answer in the minds of some of our friends, but it wouldn't be a fair assessment of Michael and me, or my marital break-up. Besides, there had never been any indication that we were anything more than friends.

"I'm at Wendy's for the time being. I'll be looking for my own place soon, probably outside the valley."

"Good choice. My place is not far from 'outside the valley.'"

"Thank you, Michael, for so many things: your friendship, your kick in the butt."

"You're welcome. It was deserved."

I laughed. "Well, I'll be going with the women's team to announce their jump next weekend at the air show in Chino."

"Good, I'll see you there. I'm going to film it."

Emotional Swings

4

A sound startled me from my reverie. I spun around to see if it was Michael. My heart turned to lead as I remembered that it couldn't be. He was gone. I was alone. Yet I did hear something. What was it? At the stove I touched the burners, moving one slightly back and forth in it's niche. That was it — the noise I'd heard! First light bulbs twisting out of their sockets and now burners moving by themselves. Michael getting my attention? Or was I simply losing my mind?

Hours had passed since I'd sat down to paint. As I reviewed my work, I was startled to see how well it was turning out. The style was hardly one I recognized. It was as though someone else had been at work on it while my mind had checked out.

Suddenly, I had an urge, a compulsion, to turn on the television set. Pressing the remote's on button, the first words from the actor on the screen were "Call my mother!" I shivered as the walls of the kitchen emitted sharp, short, popping sounds almost simultaneously, going from one wall to the next, encircling me. I instantly knew whose mother I should call.

I dialed her number. "Ib, it's Bonnie. How are you doing?"

Her speech was steadier than on the previous day, although her voice sounded halting, as if she were waiting for more blows. "Oh, okay, I guess. So much to do. How are you?"

"I'm trying to hang in there. I just had a feeling I should call you." No sense trying to explain what led up to the feeling. I couldn't explain it to myself.

"I'm glad you did. I was just thinking about you. Tom and Dale are over at Mike's apartment. We had to break in last night because the police aren't releasing any of his effects yet, including his keys."

I thought of Michael's cat, Bimba. How many hours she must have been alone, possibly with no food or water left in her dishes. I felt so unprepared for all of this. Since Michael spent most of his time at my place, it never occurred to me to have a key to his apartment.

"How's Bimba?" I asked. "Is she okay?"

"She seems to be looking all around for Mike..." Ib gave a soft sob before continuing. "But she's probably doing better than we are. The coroner's doing an autopsy. They said they always do one with an accident. They probably won't release his body for burial for several days, maybe not even until next week. Dale said he had a will. Do you know anything about it?"

"Yes, he had," I replied, remembering how we had made handwritten wills. I had, in fact, given Michael a copy of mine, to act as executor and heir to my estate, small though it was. Unfortunately, Michael had not gotten around to making a copy of his own. I didn't know where he'd put the original.

I said, "Michael left instructions with Dale to go through his things at his photo studio in case anything like this ever happened. Maybe it's there."

"Tom and Dale are going there too," she said. "I need to make funeral arrangements and don't know how he'd want to be buried. I really want to find that will."

I felt overwhelming sympathy for Ib, myself, and everyone else trying so hard to keep busy, to keep from thinking about their loss, what Michael's absence would mean in their lives. I seemed to be outside myself, feeling a special connection with Ib, Tom, Dale, all of Michael's friends. I saw what they were doing, feeling, what it was he loved in them, as if I had a direct pipeline into their souls.

Then I heard Michael's unmistakable voice in my ear and instantly repeated his words to Ib. "Please yourself. Do what feels right to make *yourself* feel better." In my own words I added, "I don't think it would make any difference to him how he's buried." Ib and I discussed possible scenarios for the funeral, then hung up, promising to talk more later.

I sat for awhile, shaken at having heard Michael's voice in my — was it my ear or my mind? It was as though Michael were sitting on the sofa beside me and had spoken to me in normal conversation. His presence now seemed to surround and then embrace me, as though his spirit and mine were intermingling. In this state, I didn't feel abandoned or alone anymore. His nearness was almost palpable.

I wrapped my arms around myself as though it were he holding me, closed my eyes and laid my head back against the cushions. It is said that love is more than how you feel about another person; it's also about how that person makes you feel about yourself. Michael had always brought out the best in me. I had felt more beautiful, more serene, and stronger when I was in his presence than at any other time in my life. Feeling great wasn't just a cliché for me. He had inspired in me a sense of connection, a kind of expansiveness that I felt now. The grief of yesterday and this morning seemed to have been put aside, like a heavy coat hung on a rack, perhaps to be worn again later, but not necessary now.

My telephone rang, startling me. I picked up the receiver, my eyes still closed. At the other end I heard the deep, soothing tones of my brother Jerry's voice. He was calling from Seattle.

"Mom called me last night and told me what happened. I'm sorry, Bonnie." He said little, yet his voice betrayed his strong feelings.

"She said she called you yesterday and didn't hear back from you. They gave Michael's name on the late news yesterday. She's worried about you."

"I know," I answered. "I couldn't bear to talk to

anyone yesterday. I'll call her in a little while."

"I'll call her for you if you like. Do you want me to come down there, be with you?"

I thought of Jerry's busy life. He was working on a Ph.D. in anthropology, was a Green Beret veteran of Viet Nam and still held the rank of Captain in the army reserve, wrote fiction, and, although divorced, was active in his three children's lives. Yet despite all the demands on his time, I was still his little sister who needed protecting, and he was my big brother whom, over the years, I had relied on.

Touched by his concern, my "Yes" cracked over the phone.

"Okay, I'll call mom, tell her you're all right, make flight arrangements and call you back." After a pause he added, "I liked him."

They'd had a lot in common. Both were tall and dark, fiercely independent, worked creatively on their own terms, were well read and articulate, militarily trained and self-disciplined, yet each had an inner core of sensitivity and compassion.

"I'll see you soon. I love you," he added before hanging up. I sat, swallowing fresh tears, wondering how long these emotional surges would continue to engulf me.

There was a soft, almost indecipherable knocking at my door. I rose and looked through the peephole to see Auntie's ample figure and distraught expression.

A close neighbor, she was like everyone's dot-
ing aunt, looking out for all of us who shared this
building. If you were sick, she was the first to bring you
homemade soup. I opened the door and we looked at
each other. We both knew soup wasn't going to cure
this ill.

Her big arms enveloped me and she shuddered
as she said, "I heard it on the news."

She had seen Michael here regularly and had
appreciated the love Michael and I felt for each other.
She had lost her husband and children years earlier in
a tragic car accident. Since then she could attach herself
emotionally only to a few friends and neighbors and to
the animals she groomed for a living.

We finally separated and stood in the open doorway, barely able to meet each other's eyes. She could
see a future of loneliness and pain for me as she had
known them so well herself, and I was envisioning
myself in her place years from now. They were pictures
neither of us wanted to look at.

Her sorrow abruptly turned to anger. "This
shouldn't be happening again, not to you. Not again!"
She stomped off down the hall as though someone had
just played a heartless trick on her.

I had come to expect sudden emotional U-turns
with Auntie, but this was the most bizarre episode I'd
witnessed. She must have been alluding to her own
tragedy. Yet what she had said recalled something in

my own deep past. Something vague and hazy I couldn't quite bring to the surface.

Coral zipped past my door, pausing briefly in the foyer before continuing into the kitchen. Braver now than she'd been last night, she marched over to her food dish and made her plea for breakfast. As I filled her bowl with fresh food, she looked from side to side, her back arched as if anticipating sudden flight. Whatever the cause of her fear, her hunger proved stronger. She ate.

Fatigue washed over me. I returned to the sofa and covered myself with an afghan. My mind began to relax, bouncing between thoughts and emotions, when I suddenly remembered what Auntie's words had reminded me of. About ten years earlier, shortly after learning transcendental meditation, I'd had a startling vision during one meditation that had disturbed me. My instructor told me that visions, thoughts, or feelings during meditation represented the clearing of stress, whether they belonged to the past or the present. When I asked if "past" could mean past life, he answered, "T.M. doesn't take a stand on reincarnation, so you must draw your own conclusions." I had believed in at least some form of reincarnation since my own near-death experience, so it was easy to believe that the woman in the vision was me.

I remembered her now, standing in front of a white manor house framed by large trees. A low white

fence separated the lawn from the dirt road. Wide steps
led to the front doors. Over the doors a cut-glass window curved in the shape of an ornate fan. She could
smell the fragrance of the wildflowers mingled with
that of nearby pastures and feel the dew on the grass
through her shoes. Dark hair, parted in the middle,
twirled around each ear. She was thought to be comely,
solidly built and shapely, her figure accented by her
whalebone corset. Her collar rose primly to her throat.
Skirt and petticoats reached nearly to the ground. In
her late twenties, she stood by the fence, holding the
hand of her young daughter, posing for a photograph.

  I was both inside and around her. I knew her
thoughts and feelings, sensed everything about her. As
I saw her in her own time, she was smiling, as was
expected of her, but suffering a deep, despairing sorrow. For the sake of her daughter, her position in the
community, and the photograph for which she was
posing, she maintained a brave face. She would find a
way through her pain, but her heart was breaking for
the husband she had recently lost. Her pride would
take her forward, but her heart would remain in
the past.

  I shivered, recalling this vision, marveling at
the alternating emotions that seemed to have taken me
over: the devastating grief that could be brought to the
surface by my brother's voice, Auntie's face, or the
memory of a vision, and the peaceful, expanded con-

sciousness that soothed me, intimating that I was connected to the spirit of the man I loved.

My crying had exhausted me. As I drifted into
sleep I chose to dream of beginnings, not endings.

Demo Jump

5

The demo jump was scheduled for the Saturday before Memorial Day at Chino Airport. The jump plane with Michael and the ten women of Madam Sally's Sky Hookers would originate from Lake Elsinore. They would be jumping at 12,000 feet and hook up in freefall to form a star. Each jumper would be wearing a canister of red smoke on her ankle that she would pop open upon exiting the plane so that the spectators could see her better against the sky.

The procedure had been carefully choreographed on the ground. Every woman knew her position and the order of exit from the plane. The first two out would be the base and pin upon which the rest would build the circle. In order to save precious seconds in forming the star, two other women called "floaters" would ease themselves out first and grab handholds on the wing struts of the airplane to fill in later positions.

I was to announce the jump that day with Pam. Her arm was still in a cast from a previous jump, or she too would have been participating. Excited and nervous, I wanted to make the most of this weekend. It could be the last time I helped the team before venturing off into my new life, whatever that might be.

Pam and I knew when the plane was scheduled for take-off and from which direction it would appear in our binoculars. The plane was to circle the field once before the actual jump to get a fix on wind conditions and allow the spectators to focus on the demonstration.

The first floater was Mary. Balanced on the strut of the wing, she bent over to fire her smoke canister. Suddenly, all we could see from the ground was a long stream of white fabric attached to the tail section of the airplane. Stunned, we assumed it was Mary's main parachute and hoped it was weighted at the end by Mary herself. I was speechless, unsure of what to tell the spectators.

Pam and I exchanged glances. She must have seen my helplessness. She took the microphone and calmly explained to the crowd that there had evidently been some kind of accident and we should watch for a secondary canopy which would be Mary's reserve parachute. In spite of the presence of thousands of people on the airfield, the quiet could have convinced a new arrival that he had gone deaf. All eyes were on the aircraft.

Finally, the object holding the parachute to the tail gave way. It dropped for several seconds before a smaller canopy inflated to resounding cheers. It was Mary and she must be alive. Only a live jumper could cut away the main parachute and pull the ripcord on her reserve.

The plane full of jumpers, however, was still in trouble. If its tail section had been seriously damaged, the pilot might not be able to control the aircraft much longer. Pam and I could only imagine what was going on inside the plane. I thought of all my friends. And I thought of Michael. All they knew was that a minute ago, Mary was on the strut just outside the plane, and then she wasn't. Almost immediately after she was gone, they would later report, they heard and felt a thump at the back of the aircraft. From inside the plane, they could neither see nor help her. If she was attached to the tail of the plane, dead or alive, it would be extremely difficult to land. If she wasn't already dead, the impact of landing would kill her.

The jumpers knew one thing for sure. They and the plane were in jeopardy. A jumper's worst nightmare is going down with a crippled airplane. An experienced jumper with a parachute has a better chance of survival outside the craft than in. Given a choice, many jumpers would rather jump out of a fatally damaged aircraft without a parachute than stay in the plane and burn to death.

But the team had come to do a demonstration jump and they were determined to do it. They hoped for the best and would know soon enough what had happened to Mary. Michael went first, and then the team exited the airplane, fired their smoke canisters, and hooked up into a star. The pilot circled and then took the crippled plane back to Lake Elsinore, assuming that Mary was no longer attached.

Once the canopies were accounted for and everyone was safely on the ground, Pam and I raced to the Red Cross trailer, and found Mary seated on the step of the trailer in remarkably good condition. A spectator had found her and brought her there immediately. A few of the other jumpers had also found their way over. Mary had a raised cut across her forehead and huge welts on the backs of her legs but no noticeably critical injuries. She was being attended by an LVN who was dabbing antiseptic on the cut and scowling at the rest of us.

"Where's the doctor?" I asked, concerned that Mary might have internal injuries.

"There's no doctor. Only me," the nurse snapped. Her scowl deepened into anger.

"Do you have any ice?" I wanted to put some on Mary's head and legs to reduce the swelling and stop the bleeding. I'd only had training as a medical assistant, but I knew I could do a better job of helping Mary than this woman was doing.

"I'm handling it. Why don't all of you just go about your business?" she shot back.

None of us moved.

Mary began to tell her story, laughing and crying alternately, still in shock. I felt deep admiration for her, watching her deal with her close call, listening to what she had to do to survive. Her parachute pack had somehow snagged on something outside the plane and by bending over to pop her smoke canister, she had created enough tension on the canopy housing to accidentally deploy her parachute. The partially inflated canopy ripped her off the wing strut, hurtling her backward until her parachute caught the tail and tangled on the rudder. She did a somersault in the air as she was hurtled backward, hitting her head and then the backs of her legs on the plane's tail section. The cut on her head begun spraying blood in her face, impairing her vision.

She had cut away her main canopy, not even knowing how badly hurt she was or whether or not her reserve canopy was deployable. But she realized that to remain hanging on the tail was an eventual death sentence for her and a threat to her friends in the plane.

As I listened to her account with fascinated horror, other members of the team began showing up. From the corner of my eye, I saw a flash of yellow and black, the colors of Michael's jumpsuit, as he rushed to Mary's side. He knelt in front of her on one knee and, taking her hands in his, began talking quietly to her.

"Look here, I'm trying..." the LVN began to protest.

Michael stood up, putting himself between Mary

and the nurse. In a low voice, he said something I could not hear but the LVN backed off without another word.

He again knelt in front of Mary and as her emotions began to focus on him she broke down, crying in his arms. We all knew that Michael was giving her the medicine she needed at the moment.

Because Michael and Mary were skydivers I realized they shared a special bond. I also knew Michael instinctively provided emotional support for anyone in need. I, too, had been a recipient of his compassion. It had given me the strength to start a new life. Now I watched with mixed feelings as he used his ability to help Mary.

Although I wanted Mary to have Michael's healing attention, I was surprised to realize that I was envious of this tender drama, of his arms around her. He was focused only on her. I thought that I might be in love with him.

I told myself that what I was seeing was simply a deep and caring friendship. After all, Mary's romantic interest was a pilot from the drop zone with whom she shared her home. If he'd been here today, he would have been the one giving her the attention she needed.

Or perhaps my envy was rooted in disappointment that Larry had not been there for me when I needed him most. Either way, I began to feel less significant by the minute. Maybe Michael was available to a lot of people and I was just one more, neither special nor unique.

Mary was feeling better, blooming with all the attention showered on her by Michael and her teammates. I determined to put my own petty jealousy aside. If I never saw Michael again after today, I would always be grateful for his help in reclaiming myself, although, in my heart, I felt I had just lost something I had probably never really had.

At the party after the jump, the mood was restrained. We had taken Mary to the local hospital for X-rays and then gathered at the home of one of the team members who lived nearby. Perhaps the team should have been rejoicing, but everyone seemed to be lost in thought. Mary's close call this afternoon was a reminder to everybody that no matter what precautions are taken, there is always the unexpected.

For the first time, I felt like an outsider among them. While they were in the airplane, I was safely on the ground. Whatever empathy I felt for them, it was not the same as being there with them, sharing their danger and their fate.

Only a few days earlier, I had ended the life I'd had with Larry. Now I felt disconnected from the friends I had come to love. I felt as though I were walking on a high wire without a safety net, alone and uncertain of my next step. If I'd driven my own car to the party, I would have left. My own thoughts and feelings were so jumbled, I just wanted to be alone to sort them out.

In the dwindling light of evening, I stood outside gazing at the stars beginning to peep through the
sky. They were the same stars I had stared up at since
earliest childhood, but tonight I sensed the enormity of
the universe through which they'd been thrown. My
hands were clasped behind me. A finger stroked the
inside of my palm. Michael.

"Are you feeling alone tonight?" he asked.

"Yes, and maybe rightly so."

"What makes you think that?"

"I feel I'm very different from them." I inclined
my head toward the group inside.

"You are different," he said, giving a soft laugh.

I blushed. His face was filled with admiration.
Of all the people at this party tonight, the one who
deserved the least appreciation was me. I couldn't even
continue   announcing. I had frozen. My expression
must have told him how disappointed I was in myself.

"Oh, my dear, you have so much to learn about
yourself."

"Are you volunteering to teach me?" I asked
impulsively.

He looked at me for what seemed a long time, as
though he were viewing a film and couldn't answer my
question until the reel was finished.

"Yes." After a long pause he continued, "I'm
spending the night in my van on a dry lake bed just
north of the drop zone. Meet me there and I'll begin

your lessons." Before I could reply, he squeezed my arm and walked back to the house.

I remained outside wondering what I had done. The words had come out by themselves. Had I just initiated a transformation from friendship to romance? Was that what I really wanted? What about Michael? He hadn't responded immediately to my invitation. Maybe the attraction wasn't mutual. Perhaps he was just being kind to a woman who he could see was emotionally damaged.

If this was going to be a romance, how would Larry react to the news? I shivered.

He used to tell me, early in our marriage, that if I ever left him he'd kill me or any man I left him for. I had forgotten his threat until now. He didn't try to stop me the day I left. Surely he couldn't still feel that way. Yet I knew him well enough to know that just because he didn't want something anymore, that didn't mean he would let someone else have it. If a romance did result from tonight, I would have to be discreet about it, at least until enough time had passed that I could be sure Larry wasn't going to be vengeful. Michael had never boasted about the women in his life so I felt safe that our rendezvous would be held in confidence.

There was another terror for me, however — real intimacy. Would tonight result in more rejection? Considering my mastectomy and all my other surgeries, I didn't see myself as any great prize, despite

Michael's theories about beauty.

My body resembled a road map with scars from various surgeries transecting my skin from every direction. From north to south on the Number 5 Scarway, my last heart surgery had opened my body from my sternum to my waist. Just south of the 5, the 22 Scarway ran east and west through my lower abdomen, the result of two ovarian cystectomies and an appendectomy. On the flip side, the 55 Scarway ran from my shoulder blades to my tail bone, featuring the remnants of three spinal fusions (two as a child and one as an adult when I broke the original fusion). And of course, there was the coup de grace, the short but ever so wide Scarway 60, laid over the remains of my left breast.

In spite of what Michael had told me, the other women I had seen him with were more "centerfold" than "truly unattractive." I wished I could measure up to what appeared to be his standards. He had said some wonderfully reassuring things to me over the course of our friendship but perhaps I would now discover that his words were hollow. Yet despite all my fears, I wanted to see what tonight would bring.

Michael left the party first. I hitched a ride back to the apartment with friends. My roommate was spending the night at her boyfriend's place. No one saw me as I pulled away in my car.

As I approached Michael's van, the scene was

surreal, like a barren planet illuminated by a full moon. Gray earthen shingles thrown haphazardly over caked clay were the only evidence that water had ever lain here. The position of his van allowed an unobstructed, 360-degree view, giving him notice of any approaching vehicle.

As I drove up, I saw him framed in the van's open door.

"Come in," he said.

I didn't trust my voice to be steady, so I said nothing. He stepped aside, allowing me to enter. The van's roof was open. Moonlight flooded the interior, but that was the only illumination. He must have disconnected the interior roof light. I glanced toward the back of the van. There were no windows. There was a neatly made bed with a flannel "throw" over it in black and yellow tiger stripes. On the floor next to the bed was an old army footlocker and a large cooler. Just behind the driver's seat was his packed parachute.

How was I supposed to act in this, his private world? Nothing in our relationship had prepared me for tonight. No matter what happened, our relationship would change.

Michael sensed my nervousness and offered me the front passenger seat. He seated himself on the driver's side and shut the door. We sat quietly for a few minutes facing the windshield and textured landscape. I glanced at him from the corner of my eye. His back was molded into the high-backed seat, but his hands lay on his thighs as though ready to push himself to attention. Finally we began to talk, softly, as if to honor the desert's silence.

He asked about my relationship with Larry, how it had begun and how it had died. His questions were probing, but his compassion eased my fears. I began to relax. Eventually he came to the heart of the matter, continuing where we had left off at lunch a few days earlier. "Explain to me why you feel so devalued."

"You mean besides my deformed breast, scars from a dozen surgeries and a husband of eight years who rejected me?"

"Yes, besides that," he laughed softly.

"The breast is bad enough, but the rest of my body isn't what you would call unblemished. Besides the surgeries, I seem to attract serious illnesses, and you can throw in a half dozen accidents for variety. Who would want to get mixed up with a sickie? God knows, Larry had his fill. Let's face it, when it comes to bodies, I've got an Edsel."

His abrupt laughter reverberated down my spine, making me jump but also loosening the tension in my muscles and easing the solemnity of my mood. "I'm not laughing at you, Bonnie. I'm laughing at how you view yourself. I doubt there are many people walking this earth who have experienced what you have, survived it all, and still kept a sunny attitude and a sense of humor. I'd say you're remarkable. Do you have any idea how the thought of facing even one surgery scares most people?"

"Well, I wasn't too thrilled about them myself."

"But you went through them. A jumper I know was told by his doctor that if he didn't have a spinal operation before it was too late, he could risk becoming a paraplegic. He's refused the surgery because he's afraid of it. And you walk around the drop zone sometimes in a bathing suit or shorts and halter, seemingly oblivious to the scars on your back. He can see for himself that you've already experienced more than once what he's afraid to face."

His words amazed me. I had always been ashamed of the evidence of my physical traumas, feeling that people must think I had done something awful to deserve the pain and suffering visited on me. Or perhaps they reminded others of the vulnerability we all share, symbols of our worst imaginings. But there was a limit as to how much clothing I was willing to wear in the blazing heat to hide my scars.

"You talk about your surgeries as though you were discussing last night's dinner, and you don't use your past for sympathy or manipulation. You've obviously gone through intense pain and fear with courage and dignity. If that isn't admirable, I don't know what is."

It had never occurred to me that someone's

reaction to my medical history or my scars, could be awe at what I had endured. We sat quietly again for a while, each lost in his own thoughts. Michael broke the silence.

"I think the only way to determine whether or not you're right about how you look to others is to let me see your breasts. I'll give you an objective opinion. Then you can get over the fear thing, and stop carrying it around with you."

His eyebrows rose in mock innocence. "There's no way around it. I simply have to see for myself what your perception of beauty is. I don't count Larry's opinion since he's got the bad taste not to appreciate a woman of your quality."

Were this a soap opera, I might have laughed, or at least thought, What a line! But he was lighthearted, if challenging. I realized that I'd had a fantasy of lovemaking that included keeping myself clothed from the waist up, or at least moving in such a way as to hide my left breast from his view. The problem of full exposure would only arise in the dark under the camouflage of passion, when clothing would be a moot point.

I wasn't fully aware of this fantasy until I was faced with Michael's request to see the cause of my fears. He'd thrown down the gauntlet. I had invested months of my life in agony over my breast, and now he wanted to look at it as though it were separate from me, as if it were part of some laboratory experiment. Or so he said.

Yet, looking into his eyes, I could see no ulterior motive. If he had tried to soothe my fears with platitudes, I would have dismissed them as ineffectual, sympathetic murmurings. But did I have the guts to let him see me? He might agree with Larry. He might be kinder, more sensitive, but I would see through that. I just didn't know if my ego could survive another blow.

"All right," I swallowed.

The brightness of the moon revealed everything, including my soul. Looking through the windshield into the parched landscape, I slowly unbuttoned my blouse and unhooked my bra, gathering up the external prosthesis from my left bra cup. I held my blouse to my chest before facing him. I wished that I could follow the river that had evaporated or seeped into the earth we were parked on.

Finally, as I had done so many times before — undressed for the cold scrutiny of doctors — I detached myself. My heart hid behind an invisible screen and I told myself it didn't matter what Michael thought.

I let the clothing slide from my hands and looking down, I saw the white-gold reflection of the moon on the contours of my disfigured torso. Then I looked straight into his eyes. What I saw brought immediate relief. His face glowed with love and admiration! In a shot I was out of the chair and into his lap, my arms around him, my head buried in the hollow between his shoulder and neck. As I broke down and cried, his arms encircled me. He held me like a child, cradling me in safety and comfort. Slowly, he rocked me back and forth, kissing my head, my face, my lips.

"I know," he murmured. "Let me have it. Let me have it all."

His tenderness left me no doubt that I was in love with him. This was the beginning of hope and wholeness. I felt that Michael was my messenger of renewed self-confidence and delight in my womanhood.

He carried me to the back of the van and laid me down on his bed like precious porcelain. Lying beside me, he cupped his hand around one breast and then the other. He whispered, "One breast is a woman's and one is a young girl's. They're both delightful, Bonnie. You were very brave tonight and I'm going to show you how much power you really have. Your courage is obvious. Your beauty is breathtaking. You have nothing to be ashamed of."

I watching his eyes caress me as I stripped the rest of the clothes from my body while he also undressed. His head was framed by the lights from a million stars visible through the moon roof. His hand caressed my stomach, breasts, neck, and face. I watched his long, shapely fingers, marveling at the gentleness of their touch. Our breathing quickened. Finally, we melted into each other as two halves finding completion for the first time. I had never known what it was like to be as one with another until now.

In each other's arms, we waited for our hearts to steady. I felt giddy and lightheaded, as though I'd traveled to unknown shores and returned too quickly. My mind leapt ahead to what might be in store for us, as I drifted off into deep, contented sleep.

I awoke with a start to the rising sun and glanced at my watch. Wendy could come home at any time. My insecurities returned with the light of day. Michael and I had had something wonderful together but I had no idea if it meant a relationship. Perhaps I was assuming more from the experience than he. After all, he'd been caring and comforting to Mary only yesterday afternoon. What if that was all this was about and I had been wrong about his feelings? I decided not to reveal my own until I first knew his.

He was motionless so I let my eyes follow the contours of his face and body, seeing him for the first time relaxed in sleep: high, broad forehead, pronounced brow, deep-set eyes, straight nose, the black wiry hair of his mustache and beard, the flare of his full lips, slightly parted, revealing large, straight teeth. The years were beginning to etch character lines on his forehead and around his eyes. He had a working man's tan: darkened face, neck, and arms, but creamy white shoulders, chest, and stomach. One leg was thrown over the blanket and lay across my hip. It was long and shapely, like his fingers, and, unlike the rest of his body, evenly peppered with black hair. So close, he seemed larger than life. I kissed him gently on the mouth. Startled, his eyes popped open.

"It's almost daylight," I said. "I should be going."

His eyes cleared. He turned his head to me. "Are you okay?"

"Yes, I'm fine. But if Wendy comes home before I do, I won't know what to tell her."

"What do you want to tell her?" he asked in a voice still husky from sleep.

Afraid to be presumptuous, I said, "Probably, at this point, nothing."

Wrong answer. His face dropped in an instant, and in the next a veil seemed to fall over his eyes, hiding his emotions. I had hurt him and his pride wouldn't allow me to do further damage. He helped me up and said in a clipped tone, "You'd better hurry then."

I wanted to protest, to say, "I'm sorry, let me take that back and start again." But I didn't know how. Too late, I saw his vulnerability. In his own way, he was as wounded as I.

I felt sickened by the distance between us now in contrast to the closeness we had shared the night before. If I could just have another chance I would tell him of my feelings for him. He must have felt something for me, too, or he wouldn't have been so hurt this morning. But I'd have to try another time to make amends. As I left his van and entered my car, I turned to him once more, hoping for a smile, but his attention was elsewhere.

Surgery

6

My first twenty-four hours without Michael was
almost over. I returned phone calls. Auntie brought me
dinner. Empty since Michael's death, I hadn't eaten or
even missed food until the fragrance of steaming enchiladas tempted me. Her sadness was even more pronounced, but her anger had dissipated. She had learned
long ago what only time would teach me — acceptance.

Jeanne, my closest friend since junior high
school, came to spend the night with me. We had probably shared more of our lives with each other than with
anyone else. We talked, remembered, cried, and talked
some more.

"After everything you've gone through, all your
pain, your surgeries — I can't believe this has happened to you," she cried. "You know how people say,
'That'll never happen to me. It happens to other
people?'"

I nodded.

"Well, you're the other people!"

"I know," I said, still crying.

"Well, stop it, no more, I can't take this anymore," she sobbed.

"It'll be okay," I comforted her. "I won't do it

anymore."

"Okay," she sighed, putting her head on my shoulder.

Exhausted, we called it a night. As I waited for sleep, I thought of our time together, Michael's and mine. Each moment stood out as a separate image, color photos taken against a gray background. I reviewed each frame until I drifted off.

Michael and I were suddenly in the kitchen of his apartment. He had converted it years ago into a dark room and storage area. I stood watching him as he rummaged through his file cabinets. In the living room people were going through his belongings.

Smiling resignedly at me as he continued searching for something, he said, "I was at the end of my life, B. If the accident hadn't happened, I wouldn't have had many years left and it would have been a slower, more painful death."

My heart ached for the years we would never have, in either case. As if to show me how old he truly was, his face became deeply etched, aging him far more than his forty years.

I felt so close to him, beside him again. He was where love lived.

We could hear a commotion in the living room and went in there as someone tipped over a bookcase and someone else scattered papers on the floor.

In disgust, Michael turned from them, going back to

his files in the kitchen. "I never wanted them here in the first place." Were he still alive he would have thrown them out of his apartment, but now he had no body, no way to do it, and evidently neither did I.

As I watched him going through his file cabinets, I suddenly knew what he was looking for — his will! Either he had forgotten where he'd put it or it had already been removed.

I woke with a start, realizing I had been with Michael again in a dream so real I could recall the words from our conversation and each line of his face. I couldn't believe these were just dreams. They seemed more real than reality.

Were we being given some sort of special dispensation to be together for a while, me from this side and he from the other? Was there some invisible curtain between the two sides that somehow one or both of us had found a way through? If so, how long would this last? What was the difference between this other side and dreams?

All I knew was that when we were together on the other side, I felt so peaceful, secure, and loved — so freed from the restraints of grief. Regular dreams are more vague, giving the dreamer little or no awareness of being in a dream. Those can also be unnerving, worrisome, even horrifying. But I was acutely aware of how distinctly real this other side seemed, and at the

66666666666666

same time of my noncorporeality.

I felt privileged to be with Michael. But waking up was like losing him all over again, remembering that I had an entire lifetime to endure without him. I could barely get out of bed. When I eventually did, I discovered that Jeanne had left early to go to work but had left some cigarettes in the living room from the night before. I had been addicted to nicotine for most of my adult life. I had quit smoking for five years following my second open-heart surgery, but had started up again after Larry and I split up.

Michael had finally admitted that he couldn't stand the smell of cigarette smoke on me and he considered anything that was a threat to my health a threat to us both. So I quit again. Now, like an alcoholic tempted with drink, I rationalized, What difference does it make? I might as well smoke.

Taking a cigarette, I found a match, lit it and inhaled tentatively, guiltily. The mentholated smoke felt cool as it found its way into my lungs. The room began to spin as they tried to reject the smoke. I inhaled again, glad to punish the body that couldn't hold safe the love in my life.

I remembered hearing about the different stages of grief: denial, anger, contrition, acceptance — I couldn't recall them all. Was one of them guilt, punishment for actions not taken? I could barely swim, but I was certain that had I been there that day at Lake

Elsinore, I would have jumped in myself to try to save Michael. If only I'd been there. My intuition had saved my life more than once. Why couldn't it have saved his?

I inhaled again, the dizziness turning to nausea. My stomach churned. I ran to the bathroom, giving up the remains of last night's enchiladas. Empty, I sat on the bathroom floor, shaking. How I hated to vomit. I thought of the time in my life when I'd been the sickest: what I'd thought was an ordinary stomach ache was something a lot more serious. Then I remembered: that's when I first heard the term "the other side."

It started with pain, deep in my stomach, rousing me from sleep. Nausea rose from my throat, forcing me to run to the bathroom to retch until there was nothing left to give up. Yet the pain persisted like a deep cramp, increasing in intensity for several minutes, subsiding, then beginning again. I downed some antacid and returned to bed, trying to get back to sleep, but the pain only increased over the next few hours.

Finally I telephoned my doctor. He gave me the name and address of a general surgeon and told me to find someone to drive me there as soon as possible. He would call for an immediate appointment.

It was a little past 8:00 on a Friday morning. I wanted to call Michael. We had cautiously begun our relationship again but there was a wall of fear that kept us from the level of intimacy of our first night together.

He wanted there to be an "us" as much I did. But he knew that I was too recently single to commit to anyone yet. Conversely, he was not giving me all of himself. We continued to keep our relationship a secret.

I called him but there was no answer. Typically on Friday mornings he was out early running errands and getting ready for his weekend at Elsinore. There was no sense in leaving a message. I couldn't wait for him to return my call. He might not be checking his messages for hours.

Jeanne was already at work but her mother Margie would come right over and drive me to the doctor. She was a caring friend, more like a second mother to me, and I felt reassured just knowing that she would be with me. My own parents and I had had a terrible fight two years earlier. I hadn't talked to them since.

At the surgeon's office, I heaved again, bringing up only bile and stomach fluid. There was nothing else left. Unfortunately, my eruption came to ground on the new carpet that matched the recently redecorated office. I was congratulated on being the first to christen the decor.

I was not anxious to go under the knife again, as six months earlier I had undergone an unnecessary surgery from another doctor for a nonexistent ovarian cyst. "There had better be a good reason for any surgery I undergo in the future," I told the surgeon after he took my medical history.

He nodded his understanding and said he would not operate without laboratory and X-ray reports confirming the necessity, and certainly not before he could get a clearer picture of my condition. At this point, he could not rule out several possibilities but he wanted me in the hospital as soon as possible. My abdominal pain aside, I was dehydrated and my heart was beating irregularly.

I was taken to the Cardiac Intensive Care Unit at Fullerton Community Hospital where I was gowned and pounced upon by a host of medical personnel. A tube was threaded down my nose into my stomach to prevent further vomiting. Blood samples were siphoned from my arm. Abdominal X-rays were taken from pretzel-like positions and I was hooked up to a heart monitor. An IV was inserted in my arm to replace the fluids my body had lost and to provide morphine to relax me.

Nothing seemed to help. In fact, my agony only intensified. There was no comfort even in sleep, which was, at best, intermittent.

"How could I still be in such pain if you're giving me morphine?" I asked the nurse.

"The problem is, no pain medication really has much effect on the lower intestine, not even morphine," she replied.

I sank deeper into my misery. Somewhere in my mind, I kept hearing a rhythmic, tinkling noise that I couldn't identify or locate.

Margie stayed at the hospital with me around the clock. Jeanne came as well. They kept a steady vigil, even though they could see me for only five minutes every two hours, as per the visiting rules. When I would wake, I would find one or both of them beside me.

"Bonnie, would you like me to call Michael for you?" Jeanne asked. She was one of the few who knew about our relationship.

"I didn't leave him a message when I called him earlier," I answered. "You could leave him a message now on his answering machine. He usually picks up his messages a couple of times a day."

Evening came with more lab tests, X-rays, and useless medication. Leave it to me, I thought, to discover a place in the body for which medical science has no remedy for pain. Throughout the night and into the next day, my mind floated in and out of consciousness.

I awoke alone. It occurred to me that while I was not out of breath, I had not taken one in quiet a while. There seemed to be longer and longer spaces between my breaths. This must be how people die in their sleep, I thought. They simply stop breathing. It's not at all unpleasant, no struggling for air. You just simply stop.

Once again, I became aware of that tinkling. I tried to trace it, my head temporarily clear enough to move the sound forward from the back of my mind.

Beside my bed, like a soldier at attention, stood my IV stand. About three inches away, the metal handrail of my bed was moving rhythmically so that it was making contact with the stand to make the tinkling sound. The sound had the same rhythm as my heartbeat. As I watched, I realized that my heart was beating so fiercely that the pulse from each beat was moving the bed against the pole. Poor heart, I thought. It's struggling so.

Suddenly, inside my head I heard a clear voice: "You have less distance to go now if you wish to go on to the other side. If you wish to remain here, you may do so, but you will need to work your way back. The choice is yours."

I was being given a choice. The other side, I intuitively knew, was death. It tempted me with peace and relief from pain, not only from my current physical pain but from the uncertainty of future pain and turmoil. And then there was Michael and the love I felt for the first time in my life. I was reluctant to leave him. I wanted to be happy, but was remaining with Michael worth the risk of more pain? I couldn't make up my mind. As a young girl, I had returned without the opportunity to choose. Now the responsibility of going on or staying lay with me.

"Bonnie," A nurse was speaking. "Do you have someone you would like us to call for you?"

What a kind way to tell me I was dying.

"You mean," I offered, "can you call my next of kin?"

"Well, yes."

"I guess it's time to make a decision," I replied, more to myself then to her, although I wasn't sure if I had spoken silently or aloud.

"Well, the doctor will be in to discuss it with you in just a minute," the nurse answered. Evidently I had spoken out loud. As if on cue, the surgeon walked into the room, took my hospital chart in one hand and put his free hand on mine.

"Bonnie, there is no doubt in my mind now that we must operate, and the sooner, the better. Your white blood count is doubling at an alarming rate, your heart beat is growing more irregular, and although we can't specifically identify in the X-rays where the problem lies, I think you have a bowel obstruction somewhere. Adhesions, internal scar tissue from a previous surgery, may have wrapped around some lower intestine, cutting off the blood supply around the bowel. We must release the pressure and restore the circulation there or I'm afraid we'll lose you."

"Yes, you will," I agreed. "But I think I'll stay. I want to see how this turns out," referring to myself and Michael. The doctor looked at the nurse and she back at him.

Perplexed now and unsure of my lucidity, he pressed on, "Bonnie, please sign the release for surgery. We'll start immediately."

The nurse held my hand to the clipboard holding the consent form and placed a pen between my fingers. I signed what I hoped was my name.

Another nurse wrapped rubber tubing around one arm, trying to start another IV, slapping the vein to make it swell. Unsuccessful, she tried each ankle and hand in turn, but could not find a willing vein. Finally, she spoke to the doctor who, like a general intent on pursuing the enemy, had been furiously writing notes in my chart and issuing orders to other nurses and technicians in the room.

"It's no use," the nurse replied, "I can't find a vein. Should we do a cut-down?"

"Get the anesthesiologist down here. If he can't find a vein, we'll do a cut-down in OR," the doctor answered.

I was suddenly surrounded by several people all trying to work on me at once. Touched by their concern and determination to save me, I said, "Don't worry, it'll be okay. I've decided to stay."

The anesthesiologist bustled in, took up the tourniquet, and began his own search for a vein. To the appreciation of everyone present, he was successful. "In no time now," he told me, "we're going to get you out of this pain."

Orderlies helped me onto a gurney and began wheeling me from ICU. Jeanne and Margie were just outside. They stood at either side of the gurney to say good-bye and wish me luck, their faces telling me of their worry.

"Do you want me to call Michael again and leave another message?" Jeanne asked. He had never shown up. "Or how about your parents or Jerry?"

"No, I can't imagine anything crueler than a phone call now to my parents telling them I'm in surgery. Jerry's too far away and would worry until he got here. Leave another message for Michael, but don't call anyone else. I'll be fine anyway. I'll see you both in a few hours. Thanks again for being here. I love you."

We squeezed hands as they each kissed a cheek and then I was off. The orderlies ran down the hall pushing me ahead of them, the ceiling spinning past my vision. At last, I thought, I don't have to go through this agony anymore. It will soon be over.

It was daylight when I awoke, not in ICU but in a regular hospital room. That was a good sign. The room was bright and cheerful. ICU had been so gloomy, with only enough light to enable the nurses to do their work.

I was no longer in pain. My abdomen was sore, but the agony I had experienced was gone. My doctor and a nurse entered the room, smiling.

"It was just as I thought," he began. "There were several feet of lower intestine involved. Some adhesions had formed a tourniquet around your bowel, cutting off the blood supply to that area and some gangrene had begun to set in. I freed the bowel and it looks like no permanent damage will be done, but we'll know more in a day or so. We may have to go back in and remove some intestine if the blood supply is not fully restored, but I don't think that will be necessary. You're looking much better already." He smiled at me and I smiled back. "Would you like something for pain?" he offered.

"Believe it or not, no. Compared to what I've been through, the discomfort from surgery is nothing. I'd rather be able to get my mind clear again. By the way, what day is it?"

He touched my hand and said, "It's Monday. You lost a few days but you're on your way to a good recovery. You'll be able to make up for lost time soon. I'll leave an order for a some pain medication just in case you change your mind. I'm glad you made it."

"How close was it?" I asked.

"Let's say I'm glad we didn't wait another twenty minutes. If your intestines had ruptured, I doubt we could have done much to help you." Smiling again, he squeezed my hand once more before leaving.

I had made the right decision to stay and I was glad to be alive. I thought of how close I had come to choosing death as a release from my agony. When I leave this world for good, I told myself, I don't want it to be because life has become too much for me. I want to know that I accomplished what I set out to in this life, whatever that may be, without reservations or regrets. From my own near-death experience, I knew that life doesn't end with what we call death. How awful it would have been to make that transition only to realize too late how much more I could have accomplished.

Jeanne and Margie came into my room, the concern on their faces now tempered with relief. In chorus, they began: "You looked so gray, like you were already dead. I can't believe how close you came to dying. I'm so glad you're okay."

I was grateful to them. They'd been with me nearly around the clock for the past three days. Now that the worst was over, they looked more haggard than I felt.

"Go home and rest," I said. "I'll be fine now. I'm going to get some sleep myself. I love you both."

"Okay, honey, we'll be back tomorrow," Margie said.

"I called Michael," Jeanne added. She left the rest unsaid. I could tell she was disappointed in him for not being here with me, and so was I.

Finally dozing off, I slept dreamlessly for the first time in days.

I awoke with a start when I heard a page turn, and opened my eyes. Michael was sitting in a chair beside my bed, facing me with his head bent into a magazine.

"Michael, how long have you been here?"

"A few minutes," he said in a strained voice. He did not look up. His hands were trembling. His forehead and eyebrows were creased with worry and damp with perspiration.

"I'm okay now. Really, I am," I said.

"My tape broke," he said, still studying the magazine in his lap.

"Your....what?" I asked. What tape? What was he talking about?

"The tape on my answering machine. It broke sometime early last weekend after I left for Elsinore. I couldn't get any of my messages. They were all lost, including, evidently, the ones about you. I didn't know about any of this until this morning when Jeanne called me. By then I was home. She told me she'd called several times and left messages."

He looked at me then. "I would have been here. I don't do well in hospitals, but I would have been here."

"You do love me, don't you?"

"Yes, of course."

"I didn't want to leave you."

He raised his eyes to the ceiling, licked his lips and swallowed. He began to speak, choked, then swallowed again. "I don't know what I would have done if you had."

He looked at his lap again, busying himself with putting the pages of the magazine in order. His movements were almost panicky. The hospital, me, death, something about all of it had touched a nerve. He looked like an animal about to jump out of his skin.

"Go home, darling," I said. "Call me later. We'll talk. I'll be fine. You'll see."

He nodded, bent down and kissed my forehead. The fingertips of one hand barely touched my face. I took his hand and kissed the palm. I could see his eyes moistening as he turned and left the room. I turned on my side, my back to the door, and saw a vase with long-stemmed red roses sitting on my night stand.

7

I wandered from room to room in my small apartment, going nowhere, trying to distance myself from my pain. Only painting brought me any degree of peace. The canvas was the only place I could create serenity. Each morning when I awoke, my art drew me like a beacon to safety from the turbulence of dark thoughts and unanswered questions.

Did Michael suffer as he died? Did he have a premonition of his own death? Could I or anyone else have done anything to prevent it? Was there ever to be happiness in my life again?

A movement caught my attention. Looking up, I saw the living room draperies moving, not in and out as from a draft, but as though someone had just walked by with his hand outstretched. In the kitchen I heard the sound of the stove burner bibs moving again. Now in duet, I could also hear the baking racks moving in the oven.

The hair rose on my neck. My heart pounded. I moved into the kitchen and saw it was empty, yet there was a presence, a feeling of someone there.

"Michael," I called softly. "Is that you?"

All the walls emitted popping sounds almost

simultaneously, encircling me. It was not fear that made
my heart beat so, and gave me chills, it was excitement
and wonder. Like a little girl playing hide and seek, I
felt that someone I loved was just around a corner or
behind a chair waiting for me to discover him. He
seemed just beyond my field of vision, beyond touch
but not beyond sound.

I listened a while longer but heard nothing more.

By late afternoon my body longed for the second
meditation of the day. I settled myself on the sofa in the
living room, closed my eyes, and did some deep breathing before beginning my mantra. Suddenly, there he
was! In my mind's eye, he appeared clearly, smiling
conspiratorially as if to say, "Well, I finally got your
attention." I smiled back at him, consciously memoriz-
ing the way he looked against the moment when he
would be gone again.

He stood beside the walnut bookcase and pointed
to the books there, trying to show me something. I
reluctantly turned my mind's eye away from him and
looked in the direction he was pointing, to some of my
favorite novels.

When I opened my eyes, I could no longer see
him but felt his close presence. I began pulling out
books, rifling through the pages. I looked for a loose
sheet of paper, perhaps a message he had written and
left for me to find. But nothing fell from the binders.
Then I realized that the message was within the leaves

themselves. Passages were underlined in several of the books. He had to have been the one to do that. Only he and I had access to them.

I knew he'd sometimes read from my library after I had gone for the day. I'd often find a book he'd been reading laying on the coffee table or sofa when I returned. It had never occurred to me to look through it after he'd read it. I'd just returned the book to the bookcase as I tidied up.

Now I saw he had underlined passages that had moved him or had otherwise struck him. Sometimes he added his own thoughts in the margins. Dozens of books had his marginalia and they read like a journal, a road map to his thoughts and feelings.

In *Dispatches,* he left messages about the experience of the Viet Nam war. In *To a God Unknown,* his thoughts had turned spiritual. But the book that contained the most meaning was *The Winter of Our Discontent* by John Steinbeck. I had purchased it but not yet read it. Evidently Michael had beat me to it.

A few months before his death, we had talked about marrying in June. On page 176, he had underlined a passage in which Steinbeck described June as being filled with potential. Michael had often remarked on my optimistic attitude. On page 207 he had underlined another passage that depicted a character as expecting each day to be good.

But the passages turned ominous and painfully

prophetic when I read on. The protagonist of the novel is Ethan. In one passage, he reflects that sometimes, no matter how careful the planning, the force of design deflects and destroys anyway.

Ethan finds himself in deep water, at first by his own design. But soon he tries to get out, to keep himself from drowning. He longs for a familiar and beloved place, Old Harbor, where the cycles of life and time could smooth out the edges of his raggedness. Or home, better yet, the other side of hime. A place where the light is given, the light we each carry as our own. In despair, he feels his light is out, and there is emptiness where once light has shined but now shines no more.

My tears began to splash on the pages. I blotted them with the palm of my hand and read the most significant passage of all. Ethan finds a talisman in his pocket and remembers the "lightbearer." Steinbeck describes Ethan's fighting the sea, his panic to get out of the water, his longing to rejoin the world, to pass the talisman on to a new owner.

How could he have known to underline such a passage unless something had told him how significant it all was before it ever happened? A man, struggling in the water, drowning. The symbolism of lights going out. The lights that went out in my apartment after he died. A place, the other side of home, where the light is given. He called the place we shared now "the other side." Now I knew. Somehow, he's come back to me in death as he always did in life—now to pass a talisman to me, perhaps to help me through my losing him. His life on Earth might be over, but he was now my "lightbearer."

I longed to call Ib. There was so much I wanted to share with her, but how could I begin? "Ib, I've seen and heard your son, felt his presence. He still exists." Would she think me crazy? Of course she would. I didn't know what talisman Michael was passing on to me. It could be as simple as the will to force myself to go on living. Or it could be a spiritual responsibility, a job to do that he hadn't completed himself. Or maybe it was to continue to love the people he had, particularly his mother.

I knew she was still concerned about his will. There might be something in it describing how he'd envisioned his funeral. Could I tell her about my dream of Michael searching his file cabinet for it? Maybe the dream gave a hint of where to look. I dialed her number.

"Ib, I've had some real vivid dreams the past two nights," I told her. "I dreamt I was with Michael and he was going through the file cabinet in his kitchen looking for something, maybe his will."

"I've dreamt of him, too," she answered. "But I

can't remember the dreams. Do you think the will is there? Tom and Dale are looking for it and so far, they haven't found it. I'm sure they've gone through that file cabinet. They found so many papers, but no will."

"It was just a handwritten piece of paper. Maybe they overlooked it," I said. I was grateful that she didn't think I was crazy.

Feeling more confident, I continued, "Some people in my art class have gone to a psychic they think is really remarkable. I was thinking of going to her myself to help find the will. Would you like to go with me?" In fact, the idea had just popped into my head.

For amusement, I had been to a couple of psychics in the past with some girlfriends, but had not been impressed with them. They asked a lot of questions that should not have been necessary if they were really psychic, and the answers they gave to my questions were too general, or never came true. Even so, the idea of seeing this one somehow seemed right.

"It would be too hard," she said. "In a way, I would love to have proof that he was still around, but I'm afraid I would get too upset."

"When I go," I promised, "I'll bring a tape recorder so I can record the session and play it back to you if you want to hear it."

After hanging up, I called Sandie, my art teacher, and got the phone number of the psychic. Her name was Dorothy. Sandie suggested I tell her the reason for the appointment so she'd understand the urgency. Otherwise it could be months before she'd be available for an appointment.

As I made the call, I realized that the thought of going to this woman was no coincidence. In the pit of my stomach I felt a tingling of excitement. The more I thought about it, the more I wanted to go. However, I was determined to remain open-minded. I'd had my own psychic experiences but was skeptical about those who earned a living from it. This was a vulnerable time for me and I didn't want her to take advantage of me by feeding me information she thought I might want to hear.

Dorothy was sympathetic when I told her I was trying to locate a friend's will because his family needed to know what his wishes were before making the final funeral arrangements. I did not tell her that I was his fiancee. If she was truly psychic, she would know that. She agreed to see me the following afternoon.

That night sleep evaded me. I was excited about my session with Dorothy and still grappling with the impact of finding Michael's thoughts underlined in my books. "My light is out. There's nothing blacker than a wick.... It's so much darker when a light goes out than it would have been if it had never shone." He was so right! Had I not loved Michael so deeply, my loss would not have been so devastating.

Convinced now of his nearness and the love he must still feel for me, I wanted all the more to be with him. How could I live the rest of my life without him? If it couldn't be on this side than perhaps it would be on the other side. I felt fortunate to be able to feel, hear, and sometimes see him. But these occurrences happened sporadically and were outside my control. It still wasn't my idea of the future I had planned for us, and I couldn't let go of wanting so much more for us.

I took two sleeping pills and went into the dining room to paint, waiting for the medication to work. An hour later I was no closer to sleep. If only I could short-circuit the memories and longing that flowed through my mind just long enough to fall asleep. Once there, maybe I would be with Michael again. Because of all my surgeries, I had a high tolerance for medicine. Two sleeping pills evidently wouldn't be enough for tonight. I poured a generous glass of amaretto over ice and took two more pills with the amber liquid.

I had never mixed sedatives and alcohol before so I didn't know what my tolerance was, although I realized I didn't care. If I overdid it, I would die and be with Michael. And if that didn't happen, there must at least be a point at which the depressants would numb my emotions.

Finally, I began to relax. It was a cold February night but my apartment was stale and stuffy. I cleaned my paint brushes and walked out on the balcony to get some air, wearing only a thin nylon robe. The winter air chilled me but the stimulation of the cold was reassuring.

My legs suddenly felt very heavy and I stretched out on a chaise lounge to rest a moment. Over the balcony railing, I looked at the lights in the windows of the houses below. All the people behind those walls and windows were doing everyday things with family and friends. I imagined that every one of them had a life worth living. Never had I felt so cut off from everything. Michael had drowned in Lake Elsinore and I was drowning in my own self pity.

In a house below someone was watching "The King and I." The music floated up to me: "Don't cry, young lovers, wherever you are, don't cry because I'm alone. I had a love like yours, you see... I had a love of my own."

The lights swam in front of my eyes. Each word felt like a knife cut. I tried to bring a hand up to wipe away the tears but I couldn't. My emotions tore at me, but physically I was paralyzed. What irony. I had numbed my body, not my mind. I realized I was no longer capable of getting up and going to bed. I simply couldn't move a muscle. I would soon be asleep out here, in the winter cold. In the morning, I would probably wake up with pneumonia, or I wouldn't wake up at all. Either way, I didn't care. The lights from the windows below danced and winked knowingly. "I had a love of my own."

I was dressed in a flowing red kimono robe for
our first dinner in my new apartment. My hair lay in
long, dark waves down my back and I painstakingly
applied my make-up. I touched the pulse points behind
my ears, on each wrist, and in the hollow of my throat
with my favorite perfume. The emergency surgery now
weeks in the past, Michael was coming over tonight for
his first home-cooked meal in my new home. My surgery had brought us closer than I could ever have
imagined.

Everything sparkled, including me. The table
was set with my best china, crystal goblets, and silver
flatware on crisp white linen. In the kitchen, only minutes from final preparation were filet mignon, baked
potatoes, corn on the cob, and homemade chocolate
brownies. In the dining room and bedroom, freshly cut
daffodils, chrysanthemums, and roses filled my vases.
Every room was illuminated by candlelight.

I saw his orange van in the fading light as it
rounded the corner into the parking space below my
apartment. The vibration of the oversized engine sent
tremors through my feet. He must have sat for a full
thirty seconds before shutting it down. Perhaps he was
as nervous as I. The scene I had set was domestic as well
as romantic, a difficult combination to pull off. He must
realize, as I did, that this was another turning point

toward a deeper dimension in our relationship.

When I heard his footsteps on the stairwell, I felt like a young bride awaiting the return of her husband after a long day at the office. I wanted so much to provide an oasis for him in a world that held emotional as well as physical hazards.

I barely heard his knock on the door over the pounding of my heart.

Opening the door, I was silhouetted against a backdrop of muted candlelight. I heard his breath escape in a quick gasp.

I opened the door wider, smiling at his expression as he took in the room. Candle glow reflected off the silverware, crystal and china. The scent of the flowers mingled with my own perfume and the aromas of the dinner, partially prepared. Bach played on the stereo.

Taking in everything like a little boy in an enchanted amusement park, he broke into the widest grin I had ever seen. My nervousness vanished as I realized my attempt to please him had been successful. Here he and I were invincible.

"I've been out in the field all day and I'm far too dusty to relax until I've had a bath," he said as he stroked my cheek. "Let me shed my day in your bathtub and then we'll have our night."

"I'll draw a bath for you." I took his hand in both of mine and kissed his palm.

I gathered a one-size-fits-all kimono from my closet and brought it into the bathroom where I began filling the tub with my favorite foaming bath oil.

"Something clean for you to wear after your bath," I said, pointing to the robe just as he was coming into the bathroom. He had undressed in the bedroom as I was filling the tub. I started to leave.

"Not so fast," he said huskily, "Share the bath with me. I don't want to experience anything here without you." He kept his eyes on mine as I loosed my robe and let it drop. We slid into the water together. He lay back against the porcelain tub, drawing my back against his chest, using his torso and legs to form a backrest for me.

As we soaked together, we were mesmerized by the faint music from the living room and the flickering candlelight throwing golden reflections into the mirror. Finally, we began talking about his day, my health, and things both new lovers and seasoned couples share.

I sponged his arms and legs as we talked, slowly and deliberately, with a thick washcloth filled with the soapy water. I turned to face him and completed his massage. After a time, we both heard his stomach growling and we laughed as the sound echoed off the tile.

"Hungry?" I asked.

"For many things," he answered. He held both my arms in his hands. His eyes caressed me from head to knees as I knelt in front of him. "All in good time," he said softly, almost to himself. Then, "But, yes, why don't you finish preparing dinner. I'll be there in a minute." He helped me out of the bathtub, his gaze never leaving me as I dried myself and put on my robe.

By the time the steaks were ready, he had reset the dining table on my living room coffee table and settled onto the floor.

"The dining room table is a little too formal for me."

I laughed. I, too, preferred to eat off my coffee table, rather than at a formal setting.

We ate slowly, still enchanted by the atmosphere and each other, talking when moved to do so, yet comfortable with silence. We had been making love with every look and movement from the moment he arrived so that by dinner's end our excitement was almost unbearable.

We stood up, each of us waiting for the other to initiate the move to the bedroom. Suddenly we came to each other, each of us peeling off the other's robe. He lifted me in his arms and carried me to bed.

His deliberate grace and controlled passion prevented a rush to our final conclusion, making our union all the more exquisite. He knew instinctively how to play me and I him, and for the second time, coming together was a mingling of spirits that seemed to encompass the earth.

8

It was morning, but the song bounced around my head like a wayward ping-pong ball: "...Hello young lovers, wherever you are...." I was not on the balcony but in my warm bed, with blankets tucked around me. Remembering last night and how I'd been unable to move, I couldn't imagine how I'd gotten here. Could someone have gotten into my apartment during the night, found me and put me to bed? I rose unsteadily and checked the front door to see if the bolt was locked. It was. No one could have locked it from the outside without a key and I was the only living person who had one.

Well, I thought, I guess I'm meant to live. If I survived last night without even a head cold, I guess dying will not come easily for me.

During the drive to the San Fernando Valley for my appointment with Dorothy, I felt as though Michael were riding beside me in the car. If I looked straight ahead, yet focused my vision peripherally, I seemed to see him talking to me, sitting in the passenger seat. I could hear his voice, but it came from far away and I couldn't make out the words. The feeling that he was near, however, brought me comfort.

But, above all, I wanted to know the truth. I felt so certain that Michael's spirit was near me and that all these recent experiences were real, but if Dorothy told me otherwise, I would have to rethink my interpretation of these events. Determined not to tell her any more than necessary, I planned to ask for specific information about Michael, to verify her abilities and his presence.

Dorothy's husband greeted me at the door to explain that his wife was "in session" on the telephone and would be with me shortly. As I waited in their living room, I looked around their house, furnished simply and plainly. Whatever the motivation was for her taking up her line of work, it was evidently not prosperity.

She had told me over the phone that she was working me in around other appointments and could only give me a 30-minute session. I thought that was certainly enough time to prove or disprove the validity of her reading, and, provided she was legitimate, find out about Michael's will. Any additional information would be a plus. In order to best use that time, I had prepared some questions in advance.

When she entered the room after concluding her telephone session, I was surprised by her appearance. She looked like a generic grandmother, with swollen ankles, a flowered house dress, and a face that implied she'd seen a lot of living. She greeted me and ushered me into a sitting room with two chairs, a side table on which rested a table lamp, and a floor lamp standing beside the chair on which I was to sit. While she was polite, she seemed to be listening in on another conversation somewhere, as though any talk between us was superfluous. It was like watching someone eavesdropping on a party line.

According to her instructions when I'd made the appointment, I had brought a few articles of Michael's to help her "tune into him." I gave them to her but she said, "I don't really need these things in this case because he's right here beside you. He's coming in loud and clear." She closed her eyes for a few seconds then opened them, looking at me.

"Oh, my, he really loves you. Oh, dear, how sad. I can feel the energy of his love. You were to be married, weren't you?"

She stared in my direction without seeing me, as she continued, "Yes, in June. He was going to marry you in June."

As Dorothy spoke, the lit floor lamp beside me dimmed, then brightened, alternately, as though it were sending a message in Morse code. I felt chills go down my back once again, and my skin rose in goose bumps.

I asked Dorothy, "How do you know he's here?"

"I can see him." With unfocused eyes she looked and pointed with her chin in the direction just to my right. "And he's flickering the light to let you know he's here." With that, the lamp beside her chair also began to flicker. My goose bumps rose to new heights.

Straining now to retain some objectivity, I asked "Does this happen often during sessions? Lights going on and off?"

"No, I don't remember this ever happening before. It seems to be his message to you. He wants you to know it is him when that happens, that he is very close."

I felt a tremendous relief, but of course this is what I wanted to hear. I still needed proof that she was really receiving messages from him. Before I could ask her for any, she said, "You want proof that he is really here, don't you? He said you would require it before you would believe this was really happening."

"Yes I do, but do you mind if I tape record this session before we go any further? I'm also going to take notes because I don't want to miss anything."

"Of course you may tape record and take notes," she replied. "I'll go on when you're ready."

After a nod from me, she continued. "He's trying to give me a name he called you; not really a nickname but something other than your given name." She began to chuckle. "He's doing charades. He's happy to be able to communicate from his side to ours, but he hasn't quite gotten the hang of it yet.

"He's showing me a jar of honey with bees

around it. Did he call you honey? No, wait, it has to do with the bees. Sweetbee? No, bee, something like that."

I felt my eyes expand and my throat go dry as I confirmed, "He called me B, like the letter B."

"Yes, yes, he's jumping up and down. He's going fast now. He says he wants you to go on the train trip, the one he and you had planned to go on together. Go with girl friends and don't be maudlin. He'll be there, too, and you'll have a good time.

"He's sorry he didn't want to go on the cruise with you. He realizes now how much that had meant to you."

A few months earlier I had asked Michael to go on a short cruise down to Mexico, as a romantic getaway. He had joked about feeling claustrophobic on a ship and said that it would not be his preferred type of vacation. That's when he came up with the idea of a train trip across the country and making that part of our honeymoon.

Again, more confirmation, the lights blinking crazily now. She could not have known the nickname he had for me and yet she'd gotten it almost exactly right. She had also known about the cruise and the train trip. How many people plan train trips in this age of air travel? She went on to give me messages for some others, some of whose names I did not know and some I did. I made notes to seek them out and convey greetings.

"He knows how much you are hurting right now but, and he's very emphatic about this, he does not want you to do anything to take your own life, even by neglect. You still have much work to do on this plane and it's not time for you to pass over yet." She hesitated, then asked softly, "Did you try to commit suicide?"

I felt the heat in my face as I answered, "I don't think consciously, but I did some foolish things that could have resulted in that." I was embarrassed at being found out.

She seemed to see through me and nodded as though seeing the event for herself. "He saved you last night, but he won't do that again if you throw your life away. He knows what's in your heart, what you're feeling, and he feels badly for you, but you must go on. Your job in this life is not over yet.

"He says if you want to talk to him about something specific, speak to him out loud. He can hear you. You're very lucky. You seem to be able to see him occasionally or hear him, and you can feel his presence. He rides with you in the car and talks to you. He's also communicating with you in your dreams. You have him both here and on the spiritual plane. Trust your feelings about what is happening. Your intuition will guide you and protect you. Oh my, he does love you so much." She paused, taking in the messages.

"He knows how much you love him, but don't

grieve for him so. He says once he's buried, don't make it a habit to go to the cemetery. He won't be there. He says, 'Nobody lives here.' He'll be with you almost constantly for the next couple of years, and also with his mother, and with others for the next few months. After that, he'll be around you and his mother as you need him for the rest of your lives and he'll help you in your healing.

As an aside, she added, "They can be in more than one place at the same time. I don't know how they do that, but they can. He had some trouble at first at being where he wanted to be. Over there, to think of a place is to be there. Now he's in better control and can be in two or more places at once.

"He wants you to know that it was him that turned the pilot lights off in your stove and oven, and your bathroom light. (I hadn't realized the pilot lights were out.) He wanted to give you evidence that he still exists. He's communicating with me better now. He says, 'Don't think of me as dead. I'm just living in a different form.'"

These words gave me more hope than I ever expected. Then she added, "I can see his face. He has a kind of half-beard and mustache. But he looks much older than you. Oh, he had some kind of genetic condition that was beginning to age him. He's telling me he would not have lived much longer than a few years after this accident, had it not happened." (A message similar to the one he gave me in my dream of him.)

"Did he die before his time? Was this not supposed to have happened? Was he given a choice at the
time of death to go or stay?" I blurted. Whatever time
he did have left, I wished he could have spent it with me
and died naturally. It hurt me to think of him struggling
in the water before dying.

"Yes," she replied, pulling no punches. "Most
times people die when they are destined to, but there is
always free choice. He had a premonition that he should
not..." she paused. "Did he jump out of airplanes?"

I had told her nothing of how he died. "Yes, he
was a skydiver and freefall photographer."

"He had a bad feeling about it, but he was a
stubborn man and did not listen to his premonition.
He wants you to know, had you tried to warn him, he
would not have listened to you either. It was his job,
and he was determined to do it. 'Don't feel guilty about
it,' he's saying. 'You couldn't have done anything
about it.'

"He hit his head on something, going out of the
airplane or from someone in the air with him. It disoriented him but didn't knock him out. His parachute
didn't open and he hit the water with a slight pain in his
chest...a feeling of shock, that's all. He didn't suffer. He
had a hard time adjusting to his transition at first, but
now he's having fun in his new form.

"He says not to worry about him. He's fine now.

When he realized he had died, he was very grateful he'd had you at the end of his life. He's only sorry he didn't live long enough for the two of you to have married."

Everything I had been tormented about, concerning his death, seemed to be answered without my even having to ask the questions.

"He's warning you that because few people knew about your relationship there will be some quarreling among others, but don't let that bother you. He left a paper for you in a brown manila envelope. Someone else has found it though, and may not give it to you.

"Was that his will?" I asked. "I dreamt he was looking for something in his apartment, but he couldn't find it. His mother wants to know if he had any special requests for his funeral? As a spirit, wouldn't he know where everything is?"

She chuckled, then answered, "He's newly returned to his spirit form and no, spirits don't necessarily know where everything is. He's not concerned with how or where he's buried. The body he left here doesn't matter to him anymore. He says, 'Tell my mother to do what pleases her.'"

Those were almost the same words I heard in my head when Ib and I were talking about his funeral on the telephone.

"You two have known each other many times in other lives and were married in a recent past life. Oh, dear." She paused as if waiting for the conversation in her head to conclude. "This is like history repeating itself. You were married only a short time to him, a confederate officer during the Civil War, when he was killed then, too. You were cheated out of a full life with each other then as you are now, but you were strong then and survived and you are strong now. You'll survive this one too."

She looked at me with sympathy as I sat there taking all this in, my emotions rising. "But he's still with you. He will come to you at night through your dreams and you'll be together for a while on the astral plane. He'll help you through this time of grieving. He had things to teach you and he'll do that from over there. Keep a journal. It will help you now and help you later."

So my dreams were not just dreams but a special kind of communication. Again, I felt relieved that I was not just imagining all this, or worse, that this was a symptom of insanity. I didn't know how all this could be possible, but whatever this other reality was that Dorothy called the astral plane, I was grateful for it. I supposed that, had I not been open to the possibility of Michael's spirit communicating with me, I might have just dismissed these feelings and dreams as insignificant. But he was evidently trying very hard to communicate with me from beyond and I loved him all the more for it.

"He's jumping up and down again. He's so happy he could communicate with you like this. He says, 'You've made my day. Oh, I guess I don't have days anymore. My todays, tomorrows, and forever.'

"He wants you to know he's going to send you someone to love and take care of in the future. He wants you to marry him. You'll know it was Michael who sent him when the courtship goes easily. He knows you can't believe you will love another, but you will and he wants you to. It takes nothing away from what you two have. It's part of your destiny."

The session took almost two hours although Dorothy only charged me for a 30-minute session. She evidently was *not* in this for the money and she seemed to want genuinely to help people learn about the spiritual side of life and its meaning for them.

I was all the more convinced of her sincerity when she concluded at the end of the session, "Michael does not want you to go overboard in going to psychics. If there is something specific he wants to tell you that he can't tell you otherwise, he'll convey the feeling to come back. Otherwise, he'll communicate with you directly as he has been doing. He wants you to stay grounded."

"Thank you, Dorothy. I feel both stunned and elated. It's as if I found Michael again."

She beamed. Thanks was obviously her greatest reward.

I sat in my car for awhile before starting for home, my thoughts ajumble with all the emotions of the past two hours. I never expected to hear such specific information. I rewound the tape on my recorder and began to play it back. I'd tested the machine and tape several times that morning. I couldn't believe my ears when all I heard was static. Occasionally, I could hear faint voices in the background that I assumed were Dorothy's and my own, but superimposed over them was something like the sound emitted from a television set after the last program has gone off the air. I had wanted so much to play this back for Ib and to have an exact record of what was said.

Thank God I had also taken notes. I looked at my notebook. Yes, the notes were there although barely legible. I had developed my own system of shorthand from school, but if I wrote too quickly, even I couldn't decipher my own writing. I would start a journal as Michael suggested and rewrite these notes tonight, while everything was fresh in my mind.

On the way home, I could feel him in the car with me as I had on the way up. Again, if I focused my eyes straight ahead but also looked out of the corner of my eye, I could see him there, a smile on his face, hands in his lap, talking happily just outside my range of hearing. This time I spoke aloud to him. "Thank you, darling, for coming in so clearly at the session and answering so many questions for me. I'll always love you."

Then I heard his whisper, hoarse with emotion,
in my ear, "I know, B."

"Ib, I just got back from the psychic," I told her over the phone that evening.

"How did it go?" She asked. There was excitement in her voice, the first I'd heard since Michael's death.

"It was incredible! Better than I could have hoped." I told her of the session as I read from my notes, explaining my disappointment with the static on the tape.

"I don't think I could have listened to it anyway, any more than I could have gone with you. But I appreciate your giving me the information. Some of the people she mentioned could be people I know, like Andy. That's the nickname for my brother, Russell. I'll give him Michael's message. What made you believe it was really Michael talking to you?"

"When she gave me his nickname for me, B. No one else knew it and I had gotten the name in such a significant and personal way. It would have been the way he'd have chosen to identify himself."

"Oh," she said. I could tell she wanted to ask more but didn't want to pry into something that might be too personal. I didn't mind sharing some of it with

Ib, so I gave her a synopsis of the story. After I hung up
I savored the memory in its entirety.

On occasion, after I thanked Michael for an
insight or kindness, he'd quip, "You can always buy me
a new rig if you're really grateful." The rig he referred
to was the rectangular parachute that the advanced
jumpers were beginning to use. The round ones were
becoming obsolete.

I felt generous as I looked at the check in my
hands. The timing couldn't be better. There hadn't been
much in our savings account when Larry and I separated, and we had divided that. Now the second mortgage we had held on our Fullerton home had been paid
off and Larry gave me the entire amount, probably out
of guilt. He was still living on our ranch in Wildomar
while I was back in Orange County in a one-bedroom
apartment. Whatever the reason, I was grateful for the
windfall. It would be a financial cushion for a long time
to come if I continued to live simply while I tried my
hand at painting.

Mostly, though, I was grateful to Michael. I had
been so frightened for so long about being on my own.
Yet when I closed the door on my marriage, so many
others opened. I found a wonderful art teacher in whose
class I was doing well, money seemed to come to me
when I needed it, and above all, there was Michael. I
had never believed it was possible to love anyone that

much and to have that love returned.

I wanted to give him something special for all he had done for me. I wanted to give him the new rig he wanted, or rather, give him a check so he could pick out his own. I wrote in a card, "Thank you, Michael, for all you have helped me through. Without you, I never could have found myself. Please let me give you something in return." At the bottom of the check, I added, "Good for one new square canopy rig," and signed it with my first initial and last name, enclosing both card and check in the envelope.

We had planned to go out for dinner and a movie, but an hour before he was due to pick me up, a heavy rainstorm hit and it looked like it would stay most of the night. Then my electricity went out. Through the balcony slider I saw that all the lights on the street were out. I worried about Michael's drive from his studio in Whittier. A summer rain could leave the streets hazardously slick. Perhaps it would be better to stay in tonight.

Sifting through my refrigerator, I found enough cold cuts, cheeses, fruit and condiments to make a picnic dinner. I put the final touches on my make-up and hair by candlelight. I lit more candles for the apartment before hearing the heavy motor of his van as it pulled up. I slipped into a filmy black nightgown and met him as he was letting himself in.

He looked at me as he broke into his wide grin

and said, "You'll be a sensation at the restaurant but if you insist on dressing like that, I may have to attack you under the table."

"I have a better idea." I slipped the straps from my gown and let it fall to the floor. "Let's stay in tonight."

We didn't make it to the bedroom.

Relaxed and sleepy, Michael at last rolled onto one elbow on the living room carpet and said, "I didn't want to see that movie anyway."

"I thought I could convince you not to."

He looked out the window at the rain that poured down on the darkened houses in the distance. "I wonder how many babies are being conceived at this very moment? Television is probably the best birth control this country has."

We lay naked on the floor close to the sliding window and fed each other strips of string cheese or sucked the grapes off stems we held out for each other. The opened balcony door gave us ventilation. The rain beating on the roof and balcony muted our voices.

"I have a surprise for you," I said, jumping up.

"My dear, you never cease to surprise me."

I went into the bedroom to get the card and a fresh candle and matches so he could see his gift, then returned to snuggle next to him on the floor. As we sat with our backs against the sofa I lit the candle and handed him the envelope.

He looked at me quizzically, then opened the
envelope and saw the cover of the card. Apparently
accustomed to receiving greeting cards, he put on a
tolerant expression that said, "Another card, how
sweet." Then he saw the check inside with the notation.
At first, he stared as he picked up the check, handling
it as if it were a foreign object. Then his eyes filled, the
tears overflowing onto his cheeks. Still, he sat staring at
the check in his hand, making no attempt to conceal his
emotion.

I'd had no idea how intensely my gift would
affect him. "Sorry," I said, "I thought it would please
you."

He swallowed once, still staring at the check.
Then the corners of his mouth began to curl up until he
finally looked at me. Candlelight danced in his eyes.
"Thank you."

"Have you received so few gifts in your life?"
I asked.

"I have trouble accepting things from people.
The fact that I can from you means something to me."
He looked again at the check, then back at me. "Would
you like a new name? One I'll give you, that no one else
will know?"

Intrigued, I said "Yes."

"From now on I'll call you 'B,' the way you
signed the check. It can be a name or a letter, B-e-a or B-

e-e or B."

"Then I'll be known to you as 'B.' Use the letter."

"I'll have you come out to the drop zone soon for a surprise." He kissed me again, each kiss leading to the next until, once more, our sounds melded with those of the outside storm.

"B, wake up! What's wrong? Come on, come on!" Michael was shaking me awake.

"Wh-a-a-a-t?" I tried to wake myself from my dream.

He wrapped his arms around me and gently rocked me on the waterbed, murmuring, "Sh-h-h-h now! It's okay. You're safe. I have you."

As he stroked my face I felt my breathing begin to slow, my heartbeat return to normal. I sighed deeply, my breath catching on the exhale.

"Bad dream, B? Tell me about it."

"You'll just think I'm insecure. I'm embarrassed to tell you."

"Tell me anyway. I promise not to laugh."

"I was dreaming that you and I were traveling in your van. I didn't know where we were going, but you seemed to. We were talking, like we usually do, nothing too important..."

"B, everything we say is important," he whispered, then tickled my ribs.

I giggled, then reproached him, "You promised

not to laugh!"

"I'm perfectly serious. You're the one who's laughing. Go on."

The dream was fading now, the mood broken by our play. But I searched for the details anyway. Somehow it seemed important.

"We drove for quite a while, then the road suddenly stopped. It was as if we were at a drop zone, people were milling around, not paying much attention to us. You seemed to belong there, like you'd been there before. But I had no idea where we were.

"You looked at me, unfastened your seat belt and said, 'Come on. We're here.' Then you got out of the van, and in an instant you were out of my sight, lost in the crowd.

"At first I couldn't get my seat belt off. Then I looked around for my purse and jacket. Couldn't find those right away. Finally when I did, I knew too much time had elapsed and I would have a hard time finding you. I was beginning to panic. Then I tried to unlock my door but the lock was stuck. I couldn't get it open. I kept trying but I couldn't get out!"

"Sh-h-h, it's okay," he whispered. He stroked my arm and held me closer. "I'm right here. I'm not going anywhere."

I swallowed my tears, then continued. "I knew then I couldn't leave, that I'd have to wait in the van for you to come back. I had to wait for you to find me.

Maybe you'd realize I wasn't behind you and you'd come back for me. I kept hoping and waiting for you. Then I got impatient and angry and began beating my fists against the door window, trying to break the glass, trying to get out. I knew you'd be mad if you returned and found I'd broken your window. But I was desperate. I banged so hard, I was beating my hands to a pulp. It hurt but I didn't care. You'd left me and you hadn't come back."

"Vindictive little devil, aren't you?" He caressed my hands as if checking for welts or cuts. He sounded preoccupied, as though he were seeing my dream himself.

I sighed again, more audibly. "I guess it's silly to let a dream upset me like that." I put my arms around him. "I don't want to lose you, darling, ever!"

He stroked my arm, still seeing his own pictures in his mind. Then, his vision complete, he turned me so that my back was against his chest and wrapped his arms around me, his finger with the missing knuckle in front of my face.

"Pain, either emotional or physical, isn't something you need to be afraid of. It happens. You know that. But you can control how it affects you. When I first lost part of this finger, it hurt like hell. And of course, I kept knocking the damn thing, making it hurt even more. I realized the pain was going to be with me a while, so I decided to make it my own. Instead of fighting or fearing it, I surrendered to it, inviting it into me. I tapped the end of my finger myself, over and over, becoming one with the pain until it held no more power over me; until there was no more pain."

He cupped his hand around my belly, still sensitive and tender from my surgery. He didn't hurt me, but the fear that he would made me catch my breath. Then he squeezed until I did hurt and cried out in surprise.

"Surround the pain, B, don't fear it. Become one with it."

I did as he said, focusing on the feeling in and around my stomach. I told myself: Michael knows enough about human anatomy not to harm me. There is no reason to believe this will damage me. It is just pain. Pain itself can't hurt me. I felt myself relax. He loosened his hold.

Then he did it again. "Make the pain your friend. Don't be afraid of it. It can't hurt you," he whispered, all the while continuing to hold me close to him.

Again I focused on my belly, the organs below the skin, Michael's hand over the incision. Nothing else existed. I bent my mind around my body, then again relaxed, telling myself all was well. Again, he relaxed his grip.

He repeated the process over and over, and each time my focus on my belly became clearer. Finally he said, "Good, B. That's it." He took his hand away and asked, "How does it feel?"

I stroked my stomach. The sensitivity from the operation was completely gone. I felt completely healed. There was no pain at all.

He wrapped his arms around me again and said, "Another way of looking at it is to see an inkwell. Pour clear water into the inkwell. At first the ink spills out, then it's mixed with water, then eventually, the inkwell holds only clear water."

***

"Come out to the drop zone this Sunday, B. There's something I want to show you."

"What is it?"

"Come and see for yourself."

We were enjoying breakfast together before he left for his studio. It had been about a month since our "night of the tropics" as we came to call that rainy evening.

I wondered about his invitation, torn between my concerns about appearing at the drop zone and wanting to accept his offer. I didn't know how public Michael and I could afford to be because of Larry. He was hinting at getting back together but I had flatly told him that would never happen. If he had put half the effort into keeping me that he was now putting towards winning me back, I probably never would have left.

Larry's overtures, however, proved that it would take much longer than I'd hoped for him to let go of me emotionally. I still feared his vengefulness, not for myself, but for Michael. The problem was further complicated by the fact that Larry was now the drop zone manager. His authority and power could have a detrimental impact on Michael who still earned much of his income there and would never want to give up his sport.

Michael didn't believe that he was in any danger from Larry but he respected my concerns. He also knew of Larry's attempts to win me back. His insecurity about losing me to Larry was another reason to keep me off the drop zone. But he wouldn't have asked me to come if it wasn't important to him. "Okay," I said, "I'll be down Sunday before the sunset jump to see your surprise."

Driving to Elsinore that Sunday brought back some painful memories. There was a pull about the Elsinore Valley that was gravitational. If I stayed far enough away, it couldn't attract me. But passing through the city of Corona onto Highway 15, the valley beckoned. It was there that I'd felt the full spectrum of emotions more than any other place on earth. I remembered the friendships made and the friends lost, the love that failed and the love I found.

That one little spot on the planet was a microcosm of all I was and had ever been. I had been accepted, yet apart; part of the clan of skydivers, yet not one myself. I had wished "blue skies" to friends who would soon never see the sky again. I'd shared tears, laughter, and watershed moments with the jumpers and had seen the best and worst of human nature there. I'd been defended and betrayed, honored and exploited.

For better or worse, it was still home in so many ways and it would always be a second home to the man I loved. Michael had once said about Elsinore, "Some witch must have put a spell on this ground. It draws us like a magnet, sometimes to exhilaration and sometimes to death."

It was late afternoon when I arrived at the jump center. There was plenty of daylight remaining for the jump plane to deposit its load of jumpers into the sky before darkness fell. I was greeted by friends I had not seen for quite a while, and as I was surrounded by well-wishers, I noticed Michael sitting on a packing table suited up and ready for the sunset jump. He smiled at me in greeting. As soon as I could break away, I walked over to him. Larry was nowhere in sight but I was still cautious about my facial expression and body language so as not to reveal my emotions. Other jumpers might notice and say something to him.

"So, where's this big surprise?" I asked, hopping onto the table beside him.

He handed me a pair of binoculars. "Watch the

jump carefully and you'll see for yourself." His eyes glowed with love and anticipation. He either wasn't concerned about revealing his feelings or he didn't realize to what extent they showed. Before we could say anything more, the jump was announced on the P.A. system. Boarding began and he went off with twenty other jumpers.

I settled myself on my back on the grass to better view the jump, and in about twenty minutes heard the drone of the airplane. I focused the binoculars on the pink and violet sky. They were at altitude now, 12,000 feet. In a few minutes the right engine was cut, reducing airspeed to enable the jumpers to exit the plane.

Soon I saw what appeared to be dust specs floating against the backdrop of clouds. Within a couple of seconds, the first two specks joined together and then the others followed to form the circular star.

On other jumps I'd watched, there were occasionally one or two jumpers who didn't make it into the formation. I could always tell, afterwards, who they were. They were either down in the mouth or were recounting their excuses for why they never got in. Jumpers were almost always harder on themselves than they were on each other.

One jumper who purposely stayed outside the star, however, was Michael. Because he was usually filming, he had to be some distance above the jumpers, or below them, to photograph them properly. He also stood out from the others because of his jumpsuit. Instead of a bright solid color, his was a black and gold tiger stripe.

The purpose was twofold. Michael loved being associated with that uniquely beautiful and majestic species, the tiger. But there were also safety factors. He wanted it to be obvious to other jumpers that he was the freefall photographer, so they would not hook onto him by mistake, and would stay away from him when breaking from the star.

He wore about forty pounds of camera gear mounted on his gold helmet, and his hands were wired and rigged with his strobe light and shutter release. The added weight made him more vulnerable to "going unstable" if he was accidentally hit in a midair collision. To me it was fitting that he should be as distinctive in the air as he was any place on earth.

No matter how many times I saw it, I was always amazed at how quickly those dots in the sky formed a circle, enlarging it each time another dot broke into the formation without destroying its integrity.

There it was, a beautiful "O" with all the jumpers hooked together. Only my Godflicker was out. With only a few seconds left before they would be at the altitude to break off from one another and pull their ripcords, Michael entered the star as well. His photos complete, he wanted to join the formation he had just recorded.

Success. The "O" shape breathed in this side and out another as though it were a living organism. They were all in now for the last few seconds. The human effort and technology that had created it had shaped a testament, be it ever so briefly lived, to the energies of the skydivers who loved their sport.

Through the binoculars, I could now distinguish the arms and legs of the jumpers in their colorful jumpsuits. It was quiet at this time of the day and I could hear faint whoops of joy from the jumpers, acknowledging to each other and to themselves that they had made the formation.

Almost simultaneously, they broke away from one another, each one flying in a different direction, staking out an area of space to deploy their canopies. This was the most dangerous time. If someone were going to have a malfunction or midair collision it would be within the next few seconds.

I lowered the binoculars so I could see all the jumpers. As soon as I noted that all the parachutes were deployed, with no streaming canopies, I breathed again and brought the lenses back to my eyes.

It was fun to focus on individual jumpers through the binoculars. Each had his own style of cavorting. Some tacked from one direction to another, hoarding every ounce of air to prolong their time in the sky. The more impatient corkscrewed down as fast as possible. I searched the sky for Michael and found him under his *new*, bright yellow, rectangular canopy.

This was what he wanted to show me, my gift to him! And then, knowing I must be watching him, he broke into a huge grin and slowly turned his canopy to show me the risers which hung like wide skirts on either side of the parachute. There, stenciled in black over the yellow material, were the letters "B4M" on the left riser. Slowly, still smiling, he turned in the opposite direction and showed me the riser on the other side. It too read "B4M." My vision began to blur as I saw his loving message.

No one except he and I would know who "B" stood for, yet knowing Michael, he would have an array of anecdotes ready for anyone who had the temerity to ask. His reply would be outrageous enough to tell the inquirer that he was not permitted to know the truth, yet humorous enough not to offend him for asking. Michael was never afraid to invite speculation about anything, but he would reveal only what he wanted, to whom he wanted, and when he wanted.

He made a half circle to face the wind before landing, then landed, perfectly, almost on the tips of his toes. His parachute floated down behind him. Through the binoculars, I saw him smile at me again as he picked it up, gathering the material into his arms for the truck ride back to the jump center.

10

My eyes opened. I saw him clearly, yet he seemed translucent. Michael smiled, leaning over me with one foot on the floor and the other braced against the frame of the waterbed. He stretched his hand out. "Come, B," he urged.

I put my hand in his and he lifted me from the bed as though I had no weight at all. I looked at the bed as we rose above it and hovered for a moment, looking at my body.

"B, you leaked out of yourself," he said teasingly.

"I certainly have," I answered. "How did I do that?"

"It's okay," Michael said. "You don't need it for now."

In an instant we were standing in a large meadow dotted with sprawling chestnut, elm, and magnolia trees, and surrounded by magnificent, snowcapped mountains. The closer hills were laden with poppies and bluebells; large protrusions of rocks were all around. The atmosphere was soothing. A golden-white light enveloped us. Just ahead was a group of people reclin-

ing among the rocks as if resting on chairs or chaise
lounges. Their attention was focused on a tall, lean man
talking to them, conducting some sort of lecture. He
was dressed in a loose, white robe of soft fabric.

Michael and I stood to the side of the group,
listening, hand in hand. The man spoke conversation-
ally, more like a good friend than a revered lecturer. I
soon found his talk absorbing. Although I heard his
words, he didn't open his mouth to speak, and occasionally, when a student sitting among the boulders
would ask a question or give a reply, he also spoke
without moving his lips.

I turned to Michael to ask how this was possible
and realized I'd asked him without moving my mouth
as well. He laughed and said, "You don't need to speak.
Telepathy and metaphoric images, are the language of
the soul. As you think a thought, it's image is understood by those who are focused on you. You'll remember specific words when you awaken if it's important.
Otherwise, your spirit will absorb the information."

As Michael had taught me so many things on
Earth, he now seemed to be my teacher and guide on
this side. I didn't have to ask how he had learned so
much so soon, for I somehow knew it had taken him
many lifetimes to absorb the knowledge he possessed,
on both sides.

I, too, seemed to know so much more on this
side than I knew on Earth. Knowledge seemed to come

from all directions at once. Some through the senses of my spiritual body, and some intuitively, like primordial truths as valid as my own existence. Some information came from others, such as Michael or the teacher who was speaking.

"Is this what we are now, darling, spirits, souls?" I asked.

"We're all spirits, B, whether we still have an Earth body or not. Some of those people," indicating the group of listeners and the teacher, "have not had a body in a long time, or what would be considered a long time on Earth. And some, like you, coming in from the dream state, are here on a 'special pass,' and possess both body and spirit."

He told me to think of these visits as a special kind of education, like post-graduate work. Because I have a physical body with an awareness of my own spirit, I'm able to come here and bring some of my body-mind associations. What I learn here may be immediately absorbed into my soul, but some of it is filtered through my mind so that my physical existence can absorb it and benefit from it as well.

He told me that I still have work to do that can be done best with a physical body, and admonished me to take care of my body, respect and value it, and let it serve me. "There is a certain amount of work we can do on this side," he said, "but it's more effective when it can be done on both planes at the same time."

I thought: So what I'm experiencing now is like an out-of-body experience, except that I'm not dead or dying back on Earth. I remembered other out-of-body experiences, aside from my near-death one, so the concept was not alien to me. Once, after several days of unrelenting, excruciating pain while in the hospital for one of my spinal fusions, I found myself floating above my body, aware of both of my selves at the same time: the physical one in pain on the bed and the ethereal one, hovering above it without pain. It was like taking a break. The pain still existed, but it was as though it belonged to someone else, someone for whom I felt great empathy, but who was not the 'me' that mattered at the moment. The experience had given me a more cosmic perspective, reminding me that I was more than a physical body with its normal desire for self-preservation. In fact, the most important part of me was the part death could not touch.

"Am I here now because of the trauma of your death?"

That was part of it, he answered, to heal my spirit from the stress of losing him, but also to continue the evolution of my own spirit. He explained that everything that's ever happened to me has been for a purpose. The road I've chosen may not be easy, but it is direct. I'm living the equivalence of a lot of lifetimes in one, but my spirit was willing to take on the challenge.

"At every crossroads in your life, you've had a

choice," he said. "You still have choices and always
will." In fact, he added, I had helped design the path
that was laid out for me in this lifetime. I can change my
mind, however, and take a different road at the next
fork, but it will not be the path of my first choice. The
road ahead may be hard, he warned, but it's not impossible, and the rewards of my ultimate contribution will
add to the continuum of life. That is why I'm here in the
first place.

I knew that despite my desire to stay here with
Michael rather than return to my body, this was not the
best choice for me. I felt I could only come here on this
'special pass,' and, it seemed, by special invitation. As
if my future were suddenly projected onto a screen, I
saw the crossroads I was now facing. To the right, I saw
my life as it now existed, continuing the journey I had
chosen. If I stayed on this path, he would be with me
always, in spiritual form, and I would know when he
was near. In years to come, when my job in this lifetime
was done, we would have worked for the same purpose
which would put us on the same plane on the other
side. By that time, I would have earned my right to stay
here. Wherever this path led, it was the foremost choice
of my own design, even though Michael, physically,
would not be sharing it with me. I could see many
lonely years ahead as I changed into someone stronger,
wiser, but, on Earth, sadder.

To the left, I could take the easy way out: leave

my physical body and continue on in my spirit form. But that path did not lead to Michael. If I ended my journey now, I'd have fallen short of this higher plane on which I would find him.

I intuitively knew that the different paths were not a matter of right or wrong, good or bad. They were a matter of choice: which plane I wished to reside on, work in, and with whom I wished to be, not only now, but, more importantly, when my physical existence as Bonnie ended. As I watched my future unfold, I decided to continue on the path to the right, harder in the short term, but ultimately the one that would lead me where I wanted to be: with Michael, having lived a useful life, and being a contributor to life's greater purpose.

I saw my choices as an allegory of heaven or hell: one path leading to such bliss as this beautiful, natural setting provided, feeling the love emanating from Michael and the people around us, all of it enveloped in a charged energy of golden-white light. This is what I believe the prophets of the earth and all the spiritual leaders of the ages have meant by heaven, nirvana, and similar concepts, but to me it is the other side of Earth's reality and a reality more "real" than earth's. As I looked at each tree, leaf, flower, or rock, I could see the vibrancy of its life, the atoms of its being, so that each seemed to radiate individuality, as if having a personality of its own. The environment on this side was all a part of me, and I was a part of it. I could feel the connectedness of everything.

I saw that "hell" was the path of lesser choice. There would be no condemnation if this choice were made, only the knowledge that it was not the best route for my soul's journey. It was a circuitous, alternate route that would gather more debris and find more obstacles along the way than the more direct "right" one. I might ultimately end up in the same place as with the right choice, but it would take much longer. I would use up more lifetimes and go through more pain to get back, and those I had wished to be with might have moved on without me. Hell, for me, would be any place where Michael was not.

I asked him, "What if I try very hard to stay on this path of 'first choice' and I meet with an accident like you did and don't fulfill my purpose on earth?"

I asked this, knowing as soon as my thoughts were formed that I was still petitioning for an early exit from Earth which would enable me to be with Michael sooner.

He saw through me as clearly as he had on Earth. With some impatience in his voice, he admonished, "Use your intuition, B. It's the voice of your soul." He explained that psychic phenomena, intuition, a feeling to do or not to do something, all come from the same source. It's my spirit talking to me, or a guardian, like himself, talking through my spirit.

Whatever the voices are, they are all aspects of the same power. Intuition is the best asset I have to guide me and help me.

He said, "My intuition tried to warn me about my last jump, but I didn't listen. I'm happy over here now, but I've paid a price for departing early. Part of the work I'm doing on this side is to make up for it.

"When I want to talk to you on earth, my words and thoughts are usually filtered through your spirit. Trust that little voice inside you. It's served you well in the past and it's the greatest ally and source of truth you have." He explained that my reasoning mind doesn't have access to all the knowledge I may need to make right choices for myself, especially at critical cross-roads in my life. But my spirit does.

"Learn to quiet your mind so you can turn up the volume of your soul. This little body," he said, holding me closer, "may think it wants something, but your spirit will guide you to what you need, if you let it. It will always take you to your highest purpose." He put his arm around me, and held me as I faded back to Earth.

Funeral

11

Ib made final funeral arrangements for Michael
although his will never turned up. She had received a
copy of his autopsy report and asked me to come over
to review it with her. The report noted a large, dark
bruise on Michael's forehead. The psychic had mentioned that he'd been hit in the head.

"Read the witness accounts," she urged. "See if
anything strikes you as odd."

There were twelve people involved in the jump
that day and there were several accounts of what had
happened. Some had failed to notice that anything was
wrong at all. Jumpers were supposed to look out for
each other and keep an account of everyone else on the
jump. Although this was not an ordinary skydive, since
the jumpers were being filmed for television, they still
should have paid attention to the photographer who,
they had hoped, would make them famous.

Others claimed to have seen him standing on the
lake, waving that "he was okay," assuming he must
have landed on a sandbar submerged just below the
waterline. To these people, he seemed not to be hurt so
they did not hurry to the one rowboat that was available to rescue him. Even the pilot of the jump plane, as

he circled back over the lake to land, had seen Michael hit the water but had also seen him standing on it moments later, waving. He, too, took the wave to mean that Michael was all right.

Still others saw Michael, with his malfunctioned main canopy streaming above him, cut it away and pull his reserve, then watched as the reserve chute also failed to inflate fully. Some suspension lines seemed to be wrapped over the canopy. But even these people did not get in the boat that would later recover his body. That job was performed by a close friend of Michael's who had been driving on the opposite side of the lake, observing the jump. When he saw a reserve canopy partially inflated over the lake, he immediately raced to the other side where the crew was camped. There he learned that it was Michael who had fallen into the water. He was the first to get into the boat and into the water to try to find his friend. By this time, Michael was no longer visible.

"I can't believe this," I finally said.

Ib and I were both upset by all that had gone wrong that day. If someone had accidentally hit Michael in the head and disoriented him, no one owned up to it. They certainly were not looking out for his safety. Where were the safety precautions, such as two or more motorized boats, manned and in the water? If, by some miracle, Michael had landed on a sandbar and was waiting for someone to help him, the other jumpers should immediately have gotten in the boat to retrieve him. It was, after all, February, and the water was extremely cold. At the very least, he'd be suffering from hypothermia. Instead, it took a friend on the opposite side of the lake from where the crew, jumpers, and boat were, to drive around the lake and launch the boat himself. When they did find his body, it was not near a sandbar. He was submerged in deep water. Finally, when his body was found and hoisted into the boat, someone started CPR on him. His color began to pinken, but because they could not find a pulse in his wrist, they discontinued the CPR. People have been revived after considerable time in cold water. But they gave up.

Ib and I were sickened by the thought that, had any one of these circumstances been different, Michael's life may have been saved.

That night before going to bed, I asked Michael to tell me what really happened, and how it felt for him to die as he did. He showed me his experience in a dream, but as though it were my own experience.

I was dumped in the water unexpectedly. My reserve canopy bobbed up and down in the water, reminding me of white horses entangled in their reins, flailing in the sudden wet. The weight of the canopy was pulling everything down, me with it. I tried to get out of the parachute harness, but everything was sinking too quickly.

An airplane flew overhead and I knew help was near;

I had only to make it to shore. There were people there but they were too far away, talking to each another, not paying attention to me. I took in my surroundings, the water, the land, the people. I was not afraid, just saddened. There was no pain or struggle, just the recognition of where I was and the inevitable outcome. As I accepted my fate, I felt myself grow and expand and, remarkably, love overcame me.

When I awoke, I determined never to ask such a question again. It was too difficult to see the end of his life through his eyes. I was grateful that he had not suffered, but I could not be objective about losing him, and the sadness of feeling abandoned in the middle of the lake was too much for me. I wanted to be able to see him as he was now, happy, on the other side.

***

My brother Jerry flew in to be with me. It was good to have him there for support and comfort. It soon became apparent to Jerry, however, that we were not the only ones occupying my apartment. I had relit the stove and oven pilot lights after Michael had extinguished them. I cooked little for myself but with Jerry's arrival I thought we might not want to eat all our meals out. As we sat on the sofa together the first night of his visit, I told him what I knew of Michael's accident and how I was coping with his loss.

"Sometimes I feel as if I'm two people, each aware of the other. One is in misery and grief and the other is outside myself, stronger, watching the first. Kind of like when I had that experience of floating out of my body when I was hospitalized for my spinal fusion. I was aware of both of me. The one in the air and the one on the bed. Do you think I'm schizophrenic or something?"

He smiled and said, "I don't know what you're going through exactly, but I think I had a similar sensation when I was in Viet Nam. A friend of mine calls it functional schizophrenia. He'd experienced it too, during World War Two. You split off from yourself, so that part of you is safe and can take in the whole scene, while the other part endures whatever it has to. It's functional in that the safe part of you may be able to guide the other part toward whatever it has to do to survive. Actually, the fact that you can be outside yourself when under stress is probably an indication that you'll get through this all right."

As we talked, the floor lamp next to us began to flicker. I drew no attention to it as we continued our conversation. Then the noises began again in the kitchen: the sounds of the oven door opening and the burners moving on the stove.

Finally, Jerry interrupted me. "Bonnie, wait —

is there someone in the apartment with us?" His hand went to the back of his neck.

"Well, I was thinking of telling you about that."

Jerry's eyes widened as I related some of what I had experienced since Michael's death. I concluded by telling him about the psychic I went to and how I thought it was all related to Michael's spirit here in the apartment, letting me know he was still with me.

"I don't know about any of that," Jerry said, "but it does feel as though there's something here in the room with us."

"Come in the kitchen and we'll make some coffee," I said.

In the kitchen, I saw that both the stove and the oven pilot lights were out again. Jerry poked his head into the oven, checking for himself, then looked at me and gave a perplexed smile as his hand once more went to the back of his neck.

I moved though the day of the funeral at about three-quarter time, as though the event had been recorded and I was walking through it, out of sync with normal time. Jerry and I arrived at the chapel where Jeanne was waiting for us. I saw to my horror that the casket was placed at the front of the chapel and was open. Ib never told me she was having an open casket. His body, of course, would be intact because he had landed in water, not on a hard surface, but I was not prepared to see him like that. Could I sit in the front pew without looking inside the casket? I didn't think so. No one else had entered the chapel yet. I debated with myself at the doorway whether or not to view his body while I still had some privacy. Then Michael's voice inside my head said, "Go ahead. It'll be all right."

I walked up the aisle, my heart pounding. I approached the casket, took a deep breath, and looked down. I noticed, first, the expression on his face. It showed serenity, peace, even contentment. But there was something more, a hint of humor. As my eyes swept across his body, I saw the reason.

The morticians had placed his hands across his groin, one over the other. He looked like a fully dressed Adam who, in trying to cover his genitals, had only succeeded in drawing attention to them. I could hear Michael laughing in my head and I had to fight down my own giggles. I thought about moving his hands myself; the pose seemed undignified under the circumstances, but Michael told me, "No. Let there be a little humor here for anyone who can see it." He was right. I felt much better for having seen him.

While sorting through Michael's things, Dale, Ib, Nance, and Tom had come upon some of his writings. Appropriately enough, they used some of them now for his eulogy. The minister read aloud what Michael had written:

"No one, no thing goes on forever. How amazed

we are when love outlasts life. We forget that the Power is the Love, not the longevity. No one, no thing goes on forever, and how well we bear the mark of where we have been is the proof of who we will be.

"I have glimpsed a thing or two of beauty in the course of my years. I have seen the long, flaming, silent fall of my friends. And their death was not a noble thing. My own life went on.

"Is death ever a noble thing? I am tempted to doubt it. But every man must have at least one noble thing to look forward to, and I think we bargain with the gods not to cheat us of this moment.

"Look for me in the people I have known and loved. Love doesn't die, people do. So when all that's left of me is love, give me away."

Rose Hill's chapel was packed that day, with the overflow of Michael's friends standing outside. In the courtyard, after the service, Jeanne whispered, "When I die, I'm not doing this! I want everyone to go to Disneyland."

It was time for Jerry to go home. I knew in my heart that he had sensed Michael's presence around me, and that he knew I would be all right. I knew it too.

Purpose

12

From the time Michael passed over to the other side, it seemed as though I were seeing life through different eyes. Nothing seemed familiar anymore. For months, I lived my waking hours in sadness, but also felt as if I were surrounded by a bubble of light and energy that was telling me, "There, there, Bonnie. You've had a great shock. Let me take over for a while. You just ride copilot, and leave the driving to me." Perhaps the "me" was my own spirit, or Michael, or some other guiding energy, or even God. Whatever it was, it was the only thing I trusted to get me through my grief.

Each night, the veil that separates Earth's reality from the other side was parted for me. The other side, I came to feel, was the world in which this other "me" operated, in which it was the host and I a guest. In this dimension I was also aware of a presence that I thought to be God — not personified, but as an all-encompassing, loving energy. It was the golden-white, almost palpable atmosphere that permeates the other side. Perhaps my desire to communicate with Michael enhanced this ability to experience both dimensions, sometimes simultaneously. Whatever the reason for this phenomenon, the blessing was that I never felt alone.

Dozens of times throughout the day, I could identify Michael's presence enveloping me with love and cushioning my sorrow. At these times, I knew it was him because I felt as if he had just entered the room. When he was alive, no matter how quietly he would steal into a room, even with my back turned I always knew he was there.

Coming home one evening I saw the flashing red light on my answering machine signaling messages. I rewound the tape to find it backtracked only a fraction. In the lead of the tape, I heard one sound whispered into the machine: "B." I replayed it again and again, to see if it was really there or just a glitch on the tape. Eventually, I played it for others. Everyone heard the same thing. The sound "B" was sighed onto my tape.

Before beginning my meditation one day, I sobbed, "If only I could feel your arms around me one more time." I was grateful for his spiritual presence but there were times when I missed the touch of his body. On the other side, we both had solid bodies but I so wanted his on this side as well. Yet I knew my wish was frivolous.

As I reclined on the sofa and began to ease into my mantra, I felt myself embraced by two arms. The position of the arms around me indicated a body under my own, yet I felt as though I were supported by a cushion of air. They were Michael's arms embracing me, for I could feel his pinkie finger with the end missing. They felt as solid to me as my own. Gratefully, I held his arms around me and blessed him for fulfilling my wish.

Michael also gave me what I called the "goodnight kiss." In bed each night, just before sleep, the walls of my bedroom, from left to right, popped almost simultaneously. Immediately following this, a rush of warm air passed the length of my body, from my feet to the top of my head. It felt as though my every cell were being caressed. And every night, my dreams became visits with him and lessons on the other side.

Michael draped an arm over my shoulder as we stood in the company of other spirits watching a Master spirit perform incredible flying maneuvers. The Master had a bald head with a muscular, stocky body clothed in a form-fitting body suit. Like a test pilot without an airplane, he soared straight up and paused in midair, turning and twisting his body in precise, fluid movements, changing his speed and direction at will. This seemed to be an unusual accomplishment, even for a spirit body. The others with us were also spellbound. Some applauded after a particularly spectacular feat. In a recent meditation, I had seen Michael's spirit body practicing a kind of gymnastic maneuver but it was elementary compared to what this Master could do.

Perhaps this was how a spirit body learned to move within an atmosphere governed by different physical laws than those that applied to Earth. As a student here, I didn't seem to have the control over my spirit body that the others had over theirs. I was being led by an invisible hand to observe and experience specific things, whereas the spirits who were here without the encumbrance of an Earth body, like Michael, seemed to choose their movements. Learning how to get there was apparently part of the process.

Or perhaps the aerobatics were an illustration of how a spirit continues to work, improving itself, on the other side. The difference between Michael's practice tries and the Master's aerial feats showed me the effort required for the spirit to learn, and what could be accomplished in the process.

After the Master's demonstration, Michael and I strolled along a path and another woman fell in step with us. She seemed to know us. Although I didn't recognize her, we chatted as if we were old friends. Soon we found ourselves in a Chinese garden. In a clearing bordered by ancient magnolia and sandalwood trees stood a stone table about five feet in diameter. Three stone stools carved roughly like mushrooms were placed around the table. A warm stone oven about three feet high with iron grillwork was nearby, and stone lanterns low to the ground circled the stools. To enhance the sense of privacy, the dining area was surrounded by large chrysanthemum and rose bushes. A few feet away, water lilies floated on a small kidney-shaped lake.

Our friend left us alone for a moment. Michael said, "Sit, B," indicating one of the stools at the table. "I have something for you." He had prepared dinner which was being kept warm in the oven. His eyes twinkled as he grinned, obviously proud of his culinary gift. He took a thick, ceramic plate from the oven and placed it on the table before me. It was laden with food I didn't recognize, but the aroma was heavenly.

My first bite told me how delicious it was. "I've never tasted anything like this," I told him. "There are spices in here I've never had before. It's absolutely wonderful."

Michael beamed. Then I added, "This is a switch, huh, darling? You fixing *me* dinner!" He took an identical dinner plate from the oven and he, too, began to eat. Surprised, I said, "I didn't know you could eat or would even want to!"

Our friend rejoined us at the table, bringing her own plate of food. I didn't mind her company. She had a happy, open face with large, brown eyes and a wide, joyous smile. I thought to myself: If this were happening on earth, I'd be jealous or at least ill at ease having another woman around Michael. But here, I felt so secure that none of the petty fears of earth troubled me.

"This is a wonderful setting," I said to both of them. "Why did you choose it for our dinner?"

She looked at Michael, then at me, and replied, "Because of some of the lessons your soul learned during your lifetime in China, we wanted a similar setting to remind you of the importance of the information you receive on this side. Also, we want you to remember the lesson tonight.

"You may have noticed that sometimes during the night you will awaken suddenly from the shaking of the bed, a touch on your skin, or a sudden noise. It is Michael or one of us awakening you to help you remember a particular point we are trying to make during your process over here. Sometimes you are too sleepy to write it down, and by morning you may not remember it. If we can appeal to more of your Earth senses, as with the aroma and flavor of the meal, the beauty of the setting, the remarkable antiquity around you, you will remember more."

When we finished our meal, Michael left the table and, as if it had been prearranged, stood apart from us while she continued to talk to me.

"A goal for you in this lifetime is patience. You thought you were being patient, waiting to marry Michael, but this was not true patience. There were many peripheral circumstances that set the pace of your relationship, some of which the two of you may have been able to overcome and some you probably would not have. True patience, like faith in the future and in your higher purpose, is something you still must learn."

I took the instruction without comment, knowing that none was necessary.

Michael rejoined us and the three of us walked out of the garden into an open area resembling a park, with paths winding around trees, fountains, benches, and tables. Other spirits were all around, occupied with various tasks. Some were tending gardens, others were in deep conversation, and a few were walking on the paths. No one appeared to be wandering around without purpose. Michael and our friend joined a group that seemed to have been waiting for them. One member of the group unfurled a set of blueprints. They apparently had been working on a project together and were waiting for Michael and our friend to finish talking with me so they could resume.

Ordinarily, I sensed when my lesson for the night was over and I'd return to my earth body. Tonight, however, it was evidently not yet time to go back. As I observed them, I saw Michael's body divide in two, each half an identical to the other. One twin continued working with the group, but the other one walked a few paces away and stepped through an opening that appeared in the park setting. Through the opening, which resembled a tear in a curtain, I saw a man asleep in a bed. Michael began talking to him.

Soon my attention was drawn to a class being taught by another Master spirit. Again, the classroom was out in the open on a plateau overlooking a spectacular mountain range. Students of all ages and nationalities were sitting or reclining on a carpet of moss and wildflowers around the instructor who appeared about thirty, with thick brown, wavy hair.

The Master was saying, "It is part of the nature of human beings to adopt a philosophy for living, either collectively as a society or individually. But on Earth, to expect certain results from certain actions within the course of one life span, is false thinking.

"There are too many interconnecting forces operating in each of us for the Earth mind to digest and sort out cause and effect. For example, there are prearranged lessons for us to learn within a given lifetime as well as lessons we help teach others. Some lessons that aren't completed in one lifetime are carried into other lifetimes. There are experiences that are meant to be cherished and others only to be endured, but all to be learned from. Sometimes a lifetime is spent building up to the act of dying, which may be the most purposeful lesson of that lifetime, for the person who is dying or for others who are to learn the lesson of loss."

The Master explained that people will always be disappointed when they try to predict, through human reason, what will happen to them if they act a certain way. "I've always tried to be a good person. Why did this have to happen to me?" is a common cry, he said. It's not that there is no answer. It's that there are too many answers that can't be simplified enough for the human mind to understand. Interaction of past relationships, past and present deeds, lessons to be taught and learned, all come into play collectively, from a seemingly inconsequential experience to the most profound.

He understood that, from a human standpoint, it's difficult to have faith that everything is happening for a purpose. "When painful things happen on Earth," he said, "we must realize that we are not being singled out because we've 'been bad.' The whole journey of the soul is about experience and progress. No one goes through all his lifetimes without pain, disappointment and tragedy. But all pain can be transformed into wisdom, and all experience is food for the growth of the soul. One of the greatest vehicles the spirit has in achieving perfection is the experience of its lifetimes on Earth. The challenges people face are what hones them to perfection."

The idea of perfection was not something I could grasp. In the sense that he used it, though, I believed it to be a state wherein the soul knows it has accomplished all its goals through its lifetimes. What happens after that is what I perceived to be another kind of existence that I sensed as an ecstatic state of bliss.

The Master continued, warning us that the nature of the physical laws that operate on earth can block or blind the spirit's journey. Every choice we make is a double-edged sword. How we meet challenges determines how easily our paths are cleared or how wounded we become in the process. Once we come to this side, the soul can review all it has experienced and see its history as well as its future, to understand more fully the next steps it needs to take in order to continue the journey to perfection.

He said, "Soul perfection is always the goal, not just for our own spirit, but for all spirits, for we are all connected. That's why there are so many souls on this side eager to help people on earth, even people they may never have met in their incarnations. By helping others we are helping ourselves."

The Master stepped aside as another scene began to appear. We saw a rope net stretched across our entire field of vision, with no beginning or end. Although light seemed always to surround us, spirits were slowly climbing the net to an even brighter light. I knew that they were working to achieve grace on a higher plane and that the net symbolized the interconnection and interaction we have with one another in the process. As the spirits climbed the rope, those who offered to help others were rewarded with a faster, more effortless climb.

There were others, however, who, in their quest to the top, knocked other spirits out of their way or stepped on them. This actually encumbered them, making their own progress sluggish, as if their selfish energy formed an adhesive to the net itself.

The net was affected, not only by what each spirit did, but by what all spirits did collectively. The net swayed and vibrated precariously when the energy of too many spirits focused on their own selfish gain. Conversely, its movement was easily managed when each spirit cooperated with others to achieve their common goals. As a result, I could see that the path of all spirits is meant to be traveled through cooperation, and perhaps one cannot truly achieve perfection until all have.

It didn't seem to matter what each spirit believed was the best passage to the light. Some went straight up, some had more of a sideways crawl. Time did not appear to have the same meaning here as it does on Earth, so there was no necessity to race one another to see who got to the light first. I got the feeling, too, that, not the route, but acceptance of the journey was what drove the progress, that every spirit must find its own path and method for climbing the net, and the experiences and convictions we gather along the way are as individual as the personalities that embroider our souls.

It was evident in watching the spirits climb, that each spirit must do the work itself. I saw spirits take the hand of another, or place their arm under another to support it if a weaker spirit faltered, but I saw no spirit lift another on its back or carry it in its arms. This told me that we can offer help when it is needed and wanted, but we cannot take the full burden of another spirit and make the climb for it. Each must make its own. Nor does it help anyone's progress to follow in another's footsteps. We cannot progress simply by saying we believe in someone else's route. This whole vision was like a metaphor that showed me that what appears to impel some spirits, hinders others. I saw this net and the path of the spirits as the meaning behind "life" — it is here to enjoy while helping others and working through it ourselves.

The Master turned to face us again. "If perfection is too overwhelming a concept to comprehend, remember this: The spirit always knows where it wants to go. Your job while on Earth is to allow it to get there. That's all you have to know about your journey to perfection."

More Lessons

13

When I saw Michael over my bed the night of his death, the unhappiness in his face broke my heart. Yet, as time passed, I noticed he began to look happier and more serene. If I felt contented and loved on the other side when only visiting, I could imagine how he must enjoy living there. He kept his personality, features, and demeanor as I had known them on earth, but his face and body seemed to become younger. In fact, even when I first met Michael, he hadn't looked as young and vital as he did now in spiritual form.

When I brought this to his attention one night on the other side, he actually removed his head from his body, showing me that the bodies we see are not who we are. They are only a way to identify the person we had known. Since the soul is the essence of our vitality and our eternal life, why not show it in its healthiest, most exuberant state? He could still be a tease as he had been on earth, or sedate if the mood struck him, but I never again saw him unhappy. He had found the peace I had prayed would come to both of us.

One night, I found myself over there, seemingly without Michael's assistance. Looking around, I found him standing with a group around what that looked like a mockup of a city, or of several cities. He seemed to be leading a discussion. He was so engrossed that he didn't seem to notice I was there.

I had not thought that coming to the other side was something I could do on my own. Yet I had arrived here apparently without help. I didn't feel slighted by Michael's lack of attention, however. I knew he was doing good work, even if I didn't understand what it was. Michael had always tried to do his best for others. It made sense that he would continue his efforts on the other side.

By now, I looked forward to the teachings of the Masters. I looked around and saw the beauty of nature everywhere, but I noticed this time that there were also buildings of every possible architectural design. Some stood on their own, like the curving, sleek, granite structure I saw on top of a hill. It reminded me of a very thick paper clip, partially opened at one end, the flat side resting on the ground and the curved sides sweeping up and around itself at a forty-five-degree angle.

Spirits were entering or leaving other buildings that were grouped into communities of similar architecture such as colonial, Mediterranean, craftsman, or Cape Cod. Other groups had formed in a nearby park. Still others sat in a clearing in a less manicured, more natural setting.

It occurred to me then that in different settings

people may be taught different lessons. Perhaps everyone goes to the setting that most attracts them, or, as in my case, goes where they are drawn to hear the lesson most pertinent to them.

Inside a colonnaded structure that had a Greek or Roman influence were anterooms, all in white marble. A long hallway opened onto a small outdoor amphitheater with tiered marble seating surrounding a grass stage. I laughed to myself, thinking, Even when I go into a building, I find myself outdoors. A class was in session. I stood for a while watching a middle-aged, blond woman speaking, center stage, to the audience.

"One of the laws of nature is choice — free will. It's one of the things that makes life challenging. Your Earth mind has the choice to listen to your spirit or to ignore it. When you block or disregard it, you can impede your own progress and learning, making your life more difficult and less fulfilling than it needs to be."

An older man, about sixty, with thick white hair, asked from the front row, "If the purpose of our spirit is to guide us to do what's best, what about people, truly malevolent beings, who do harm to others? Is their guiding spirit telling them to do those things?"

The Master answered, "A spirit always operates from love for the soul's greatest good. Sometimes, however, people can become malevolent from habitually disregarding the guidance of their spirit, like a child growing up in a world without the influence of a loving parent or guardian. Conversely, someone who has ignored his own spirit and done harm to others, is capable of rediscovering his soul, and changing. Once someone has truly experienced his or her own spirit, they can never intentionally do harm to others again."

The white-haired gentleman then asked, "Well, can the spirit do unintentional harm?"

The Master replied that sometimes a spirit returns to earth prematurely, before it has fully processed its experience from a previous incarnation. In those cases, the spirit can become troubled and create disharmony, not only in its own life, but in others' lives as well. A troubled spirit is not the best source of guidance, even for it's own Earth body. When that happens it's best to call upon a higher, more evolved spirit, a guardian spirit, to guide the person through his or her lifetime. She warned, however, that troubled spirits need to take care to call only upon a higher spirit of light and love, or they might attract to themselves other troubled spirits.

Occasionally, she added, the spirit itself recognizes that it has returned too soon and chooses to return to the other side to learn more before reentering the Earth plane again.

"You mean by suicide?" asked a middle-aged woman, who looked around as if embarrassed by her question.

The Master answered, "Direct suicide is a human action, not a spiritual one, and is almost always for the wrong reasons." She told us that usually suicide is an attempt to find release from pain. But sometimes it happens that from the very pain a person is suffering, the greatest lesson is learned. Cutting the process short usually means the pain will only have to be endured again sometime in the future or the soul's progress will be stymied. "Miracles come to those who endure."

She told us how a spirit could manufacture a set of circumstances so that its Earth body dies from an accident or fatal illness, in order to cut short that particular lifetime. Sometimes it may choose to die in infancy or in the womb. In these cases, the circumstances are in harmony with the soul's greater purpose.

For the first time I interrupted the Master. "When someone you love dies, how do you know whether he died when he was supposed to or if he changed his mind about completing that lifetime?" I was thinking of Michael and for the first time on the other side, I felt apprehensive. I wondered if he had left early because he had chosen to do so, but didn't want me to know this. He had told me that he hadn't listened to his own intuition; if he had, his life would have been saved. Maybe this was part of the truth, but not all of it. Maybe he was given a choice at the time and didn't want me to know that he wanted to go.

The Master looked at me with compassion. "Remember, Bonnie, you're over here to learn and resolve your grief. This is also a place to heal. In answer to your question — you don't know. It is not for *you* to know. It's only for the spirit that is directly involved to know. All you can do is have faith that despite the loss you feel as a result of other people's choices, the love of one spirit for another is eternal. You don't have to grieve because a scene in a play has been rewritten. The play goes on and there are no endings."

I walked a few steps closer to the Master and the rest of the group. A girl in her teens looked at me and moved her skirt to clear a seat next to her. She smiled, then returned her gaze to the Master. Her manner assured me I was in the company of friends. The Master continued.

"The only thing worse than impeding your own spiritual progress is impeding others'. Your free will allows you to choose how you take your journey through life, but when your choices and deeds negatively affect the progress of others, your journey has gone backwards." She explained how, if we cause the loss of another's property, we can delay the fulfillment of his life's purpose by the time and energy it takes him to regain what may have been necessary to his life plan. If we take his life, the same principle holds, only a thousandfold. He must then wait for another body and another set of prearranged circumstances to enable him to learn the lessons he needs — lessons he was supposed to have learned during his previous lifetime.

"The irony," she said, "is that the selfish soul thinks it can serve itself best by taking from others, rather than by doing its own work. Once over here, of course, it realizes what its short cut has cost it, as well as those from whom it has taken."

A young man with an angular face mused, "I've come here many times between lifetimes and some things seem never to change. So many times my Earth life has been interrupted like that. I think I've learned how to listen to my spirit, but I've still fallen to those who don't listen to their own."

The Master nodded gravely, then said, "Perhaps that lesson is no longer for you, but for them — to learn through your death. The impediment to their own spiritual progression is far greater for having created the pain, than for you, who suffered from it. Look into your own history to discover the lesson and who it's for. You are here to learn to help others as well as yourself, even your murderers."

On another train of thought, she told us that the Earth plane has gone through a history of growth through leadership in all areas of life: a few people making the decisions for the many. Some leaders may be inspired by genuine goodness and spiritual wisdom, but others are motivated only by their self-serving egos. She explained that the earth is in a critical period in its evolution. Pollution and contamination threaten it. Resources are being used extravagantly. With no spiritual awareness of the consequences of their actions, too many people are concerned only with self-gratification or the easing of their individual lives at the expense of the continuum of life on earth.

She continued, "The spiritual world can no longer afford the time it would take to change the many through their leadership. Progress on Earth is proceeding at a crawl. The continuation of the Earth plane is very important to the spiritual growth of us all. Earth is a learning field without which all of our spiritual progress may be greatly inhibited."

She said then that each spirit must become its own leader, take control of and responsibility for its own spiritual progress, receive guidance from other spirits, and allow others the same freedom. By doing so we needn't be misguided by those who lead in the wrong direction. By listening to our own guided wisdom, we can solve even the most complex problems because each person doing his or her own job spiritually can do far more than one divine leader trying to do the work for many.

A freckled boy of about ten asked, "But isn't that what priests and ministers do, show us the best way? If we can do it ourselves, do we need them?"

"You needn't turn away from the religions of the world if, through your faith, your own spirit is nurtured and allowed to follow its own journey." Religion, she told us, may be spiritually inspired, but inspiration is always filtered through the interpretation of human minds, and no one mind has all the answers. When someone teaches that his vision of the universe is the only truth, his followers can become stunted with no opportunity to express their own spirituality. Whenever others instruct us to believe only as they do, without allowing us spiritual freedom, there is another agenda behind their instructions that is not to our benefit.

She said, "You will know when they are operating for your good when they inspire, not impede; guide, not direct; teach, not dictate. As you become a more direct channel for the guidance of your own spirit you will serve the greater plan for all of life."

She also told us that we can be spiritual channels to relay messages to others. When we feel strongly that we have something of importance to pass on to someone, we should do so. She warned us, however, to avoid any expectation of that person's accepting the message. He may act upon the information immediately, years later, or not at all. But what we say to him may be precisely what he needs to hear at that moment, and we may be the messenger intended to deliver it.

I heard a soft "Yeah" from someone in the audience, followed by muffled giggles. The Master heard it, too. She pursed her lips, waved a finger in mock admonishment and said, "Don't get carried away, however, thinking that *anything* that comes out of your mouth is spiritually inspired, or become so pompous as to think only you have all the answers. The information is there for anyone who chooses to be open to it. The great inhibitor of direct, spiritual guidance is the mistaken belief that there is a single religion or philosophy that gives followers the inside track to spiritual utopia. The truth is, there is no absolute truth as the human mind understands it, and no one religion is more right than another."

Now she held out her hands in which were an assortment of varicolored, multifaceted gems which she let fall to the ground. We all moved closer for a better look. Each gem had landed in a different position. She used the analogy of the gems to show that if the top of each gem were its eyes, it could see only what was in front of it. Its perception could be viewed in terms of hue, value, and angle. Part of the gem is in shadow, part in the light, which could be defined as truth. Because each gem landed differently, each reflects the light differently and in a different hue.

"We are like these gems, able to see only what is in front of us, in any one lifetime," she said. To us, that is the truth. Since each gem is different and perceives the light differently, each gem's truth is valid, but not complete. Yet the light is so much more than what we perceive it to be. It doesn't change; only the angle from which it is viewed changes.

"When we have served our purpose, we are gathered into the light again, later to be sent back to Earth, landing again at different angles to reflect the light from another perspective."

What's important, she told us, is what is true for us during a given lifetime. We only have pieces of the puzzle of what life's about. The larger picture with all the pieces is being guided by the light, the power that creates all life. However smoothly and coherently that picture forms is dependent on the free choices every individual makes.

From behind me, another spirit asked, "How would we know to recognize a truth that pertains to us, versus simply hearing someone else's ideas, his or her truth, which may not be ours?"

Wisdom intended for us, she said, can come in a variety of packages: from a dream, meditation, a passage in a book, dialogue from a play, a feeling, a vision, or conversation. When coming from others, a truth spoken for our benefit can come from a child or a homeless indigent just as likely as it can come from a renowned philosopher or world leader. Guardian spirits come in all forms, in either earthly or spiritual bodies, and often at unexpected times. We're all capable of giving and receiving guidance from this side because it comes from the source that unites us all. We shouldn't disregard the information because it comes from someone our human mind tells us is inferior. Spiritually, we are all important.

"You'll know the information is offered spiritually when a feeling within you tells you to pay close attention to the message. You may feel chills go through your body, the impact of the words may stop all other thought, or you may feel that you've just heard a fitting reply to a question you've had on your mind. You may awaken from a dream or meditation with a feeling of contentment and completion, or that some imminent action from you is required. These are clues that your spirit is talking to you, giving you the help you need.

A bouquet of flowers appeared in her hands: daisies, chrysanthemums, morning glories, roses, lilies, and others. She picked a yellow rose from her bouquet and gave it to the white-haired man in the front row as she continued speaking.

"Everyone has something to give to life and the choice of whether to give it and in what form." She picked a daisy from her bouquet and handed it to another student, and continued to give her flowers away until all but one was gone.

"The important thing to remember is that it is yours to give. Don't let others, or your own fears, prevent your giving, and don't impede others' in their giving. Only the individual knows what his or her gift is and in what form. Ask your spirit to guide you and have the faith to follow its guidance."

She had worked her way up the steps until she came to me. She held out her last blossom, a lily-of-the-valley, offering it to me. "Then," she continued, "you will have accomplished your own spiritual goal."

The Trip

14

The lessons I was taught on the other side were imprinted on my being each night and, during the day, opportunities to apply them began to occur. One night I had a vivid dream in which I was with family members who were not my own. I felt caught in a conflict between my husband and my son. I could see both points of view, but knew the right choice lay with my son on this particular issue. If I supported him in what he wanted, it would eventually lead to greater things for him. My husband would eventually come around to see this, although he couldn't see it now.

When I awoke, I felt as I always did when coming back from the other side, that I had been given valuable instruction, but this time I had no idea how to apply it. I had neither husband nor son so I could not relate it directly.

Later that morning I attended my art class. During our break, I had an overwhelming urge to tell Margaret, a classmate, about my dream. She instantly flushed as I described the details of the conflict. When I finished, I told her I didn't know why I was telling her all that, but it felt like it was the right thing to do.

"I know why you're telling me, Bonnie. The

dream was meant for me. You've just related exactly what I have been going through with my family. I've been upset for days, not knowing what to do. Somehow the answer to the problem was given to you so you could give it to me." She embraced me in gratitude and I felt a chill of confirmation that I had accomplished a spiritual channeling to help her. I did not have to go into a trance or leave my body to let another spirit enter it in order to speak through me (not that I would know how to do either one). Just following my impulse to say what I said, to say it when I said it, and to say it to whom I said it, accomplished the goal.

On another occasion, I was in Kathy's salon when a customer who knew me asked how I was doing. My response normally would have been to thank her for her inquiry and tell her I was getting along fine, no matter how I was feeling. Most times, such questions are simply a courtesy and people would rather not be burdened with your troubles. This time, however, I felt compelled to tell her about some of the experiences I'd had, attesting to Michael's continued existence. This was not information I was comfortable sharing with people I was close to, much less with casual acquaintances. Surely she'd think I was a nut. Yet the compulsion to confide in her was so strong, I couldn't ignore it, and I heard myself say, "You're going to think I'm crazy, but..," and I began telling her about some of my experiences.

I could hardly believe that I was telling her about the lights dimming around me, seeing Michael, hearing him in the kitchen. She took it all in and when I was finished, she said, "I've never told anyone this, but I've had similar experiences."

She'd had a son, Jeff, who had died in an accident in his mid-twenties. As devastating as his loss was for her and her husband, their younger daughter was inconsolable. She had adored her big brother.

Shortly after his death, the family was gathered in their living room, crying and reminiscing about him, when a feeling of complete peace inexplicably came over them. The tears dried on their faces and the music from the stereo abruptly stopped. In the silence they all looked at each other, and smiled. They felt a tremendous surge of love, like a great wave, and felt, too, Jeff's presence.

Late that night, they were awakened by their daughter's excited voice calling them to her room. They thought she'd had a bad dream and immediately rushed to her only to find her sitting up in bed, joyous.

"He was here, Jeff was just here, I saw him," she cried, pointing to where he had stood. "He said not to worry about him, he was fine and he loves us, and he said he knows how much we love him. He told me not to feel bad for losing him because I really hadn't. I could see him and hear him just like I can you."

Her parents looked down at their elated daughter and knew something remarkable had happened, but frankly didn't know how much to believe.

"And you know what else, mom?" she continued. "You know how Jeff loved beer? He had a can in his hand while he was talking to me. He drank it and put the can in the trash basket."

Her mother looked into the basket and saw an empty can of her son's favorite brand of beer. She looked at the elation on her daughter's face and knew in her heart that her daughter did have a visitation from Jeff.

She ended her story the way I'd begun mine. "You may think I'm crazy..." Then she looked at me and smiled. "No, I guess you don't. I've always been afraid no one would understand. It feels so good to talk to someone who does. There are things that happen that we can't explain, but like you, I know my son still exists."

***

For over three years, the property I had owned with Larry had not sold. I had changed real estate companies, reduced the asking price, run ads myself, but there were few qualified buyers at a time when mortgage interest rates averaged nineteen percent. It had been an area of frustration for Michael and me for a long time. We had wanted to take my half of the equity, combine it with his savings, and buy a house together. It would mean the severing of the last ties I had to Larry.

I no longer cared about buying a house. Now I just wanted to get on with my life. I intended to use the equity from the sale as a nest egg for my future alone. But within a few months of Michael's passing, everything came together and a bona fide buyer appeared to purchase the property. Interest rates had not changed, yet ours was the first piece of real estate to sell in the Elsinore Valley in four years. I believe my angel, Michael, had a hand in resolving this for me.

At the same time that the sale of the property was going through, two girlfriends, separately and without knowing each other, approached me about traveling to England with them. I had always loved the idea of traveling and Michael had even told me, through the psychic, to take the train trip with girl friends that he and I had planned. We could do a lot of traveling through the United Kingdom by train. The idea appealed to me and the "coincidence" of having two friends approach me about a trip to the same place was not lost on me. After I introduced them to each other, we all decided to go together. The fourth member of the party would be Michael.

Sandie and Sheila and I purchased Britrail Passes and made reservations at a small bed-and-breakfast inn in the south of England. This would be our home base.

Scotland and Wales would also be on our itinerary. An astounding phenomenon began to occur shortly after we arrived in England.

On board the trains, I found that I could close my eyes and see the same people in the compartment that I'd noticed with my eyes open, but when I closed my eyes, there was an additional person. The space beside me would somehow open up to adjust for Michael, no matter where I was sitting.

In the spiritual dimension, Michael held my hand and played gently with my fingers while talking and laughing with me. I could hear his voice even if I couldn't hear clearly all of his words. He spoke in such a fun-filled witty manner, I knew he was having a great time, and so was I. He would tell me about the other passengers in the compartment, their destinations and what they would be doing when they got there.

On one trip, he pointed out a rather staid-looking gentleman across from us and told me he was on his way to meet his mistress. His demeanor looked so unlikely for such an escapade, I couldn't help but giggle. The people around me probably thought I was asleep and having a funny dream. I didn't know if all that Michael was telling me was factual or just story-telling but it didn't matter. We were having fun on our train ride together.

I had wanted Wales to be a part of our itinerary because of Michael's Welsh heritage. We found this

country absolutely enchanting. One of the highlights of
the trip was a night we spent in a castle. The castle
interior had been converted to accommodate guests
with the comforts of a small hotel, including indoor
plumbing, but it still retained the flavor of earlier centuries. On the night of our arrival we were treated to a
Renaissance feast in the lower chambers.

We ate a delicious barley soup directly from the
bowl, and ate everything else with our hands. We broke
off hunks of bread as it went around the table, and
devoured roasted chicken cooked on a spit. The bever-
age was mead, drunk from pewter goblets. Madrigal
singers and clog dancers entertained us. Candles alone
illuminated the room.

Michael sat next to me throughout the evening,
enjoying it as much as I. This time I felt more than his
energy. With my eyes open and my mind awake, I felt
his arm around my shoulders. To be sure it was him, I
checked the others sitting near to me to be certain no
Earth person was taking liberties.

After dinner, my friends and I explored the
halls and anterooms of the castle, taking in the historic
accoutrements. Sandie and Sheila had become quiet
after dinner, and as we wandered from room to room,
they would occasionally look at me with raised eyebrows, then each other. Finally, we retired to our room.
They knew about Michael's death, of course, and I had
told them before the trip that I felt him around me

much of the time. We'd not discussed him since we arrived in England but they now felt compelled to bring up the subject. It seems that on this night they "saw" him as well.

As we sat on our beds talking, they both told me they had noticed a glow beside me as we walked through the castle, and they could still see it. They'd been trying to figure out if it could be coming from a light source somewhere but had been unable to find one. The light simply stood by itself, and moved on its own. They also said they felt the presence of someone else with us and asked me if I did.

Yes, said. I'd been feeling Michael around me all night, literally. I felt that he'd been enjoying the evening along with us. They didn't seem frightened, just curious and a bit awestruck, although they admitted that it was a little strange to feel and see the presence of a spirit. They felt no threat, only benevolence, and even a sense of protection. If my past explanations of Michael's presence had ever triggered skepticism, that was no longer the case. As a matter of fact, toward the end of our trip, both felt that it was by Michael's design that they had come with me on this vacation.

When we returned home and had our pictures from the trip developed, we noticed a white "cloud" in many of the photos, no matter whose camera had been used to take it, especially in those shots in which I appeared.

Nance

15

Michael had told me on my first visit to the other side that he would bring me information about a previous life together. Ironically, the messenger he chose for the task would be the woman who had been my greatest rival for his love.

Nance and Michael had had an intense, on-again-off-again relationship spanning more than a decade. She, too, was a skydiver and at the time I entered Michael's life, their romance seemed to have reached its end. She was involved with another jumper, Ed, a marine who adored her. They had been together for two years, and to Ed it was time to make a commitment to marriage. I hadn't known Nance well during my time at Elsinore, but I had thought that if she and Michael hadn't married in the ten years of their relationship, they probably never would. However, the prospect of marriage to Ed brought Nance's unresolved feelings for Michael to the fore. She came back into his life when he and I were the most vulnerable.

The love Michael and I shared was birthed in uncertainty and insecurity. He was nearing forty and had never married. Although he had loved a few women in the past, he knew himself well enough to know what kind of match would work for him in a committed relationship. He told me that he simply hadn't found that match before meeting me. Yet I was too newly out of my own marriage for either of us to be certain, without the test of time, that ours was a love that would last.

Nance was as tall and statuesque as I was small and slight. She carried herself with Jane Russell-like ease, and, like that actress, she was endowed with wavy, black hair and a curvaceous figure. At her best, she was kind and generous, especially to those who befriended her. Yet she could be fiery and sharp-tongued to those who slighted or tried to demean her. Her fearless athleticism was matched by her intelligence and quick wit. In many ways, she seemed to be a better companion for Michael than I, but they did not always bring out the best in each other. Michael had taught me that it makes no difference how good the parts are, if together they don't make a better whole.

For a time, Nance and others were in Michael's life and I, too, dated other men. However, As Michael and I grew more confident of our future together other lovers dropped away. Nance would probably always love him, but in her heart, she, too, knew that a permanent relationship between them was not possible.

Their bond was a special one, however, as shown by the means by which she learned of his passing. She had been an army reservist for years and was away at a reserve meeting in Indiana when he died. Without anyone calling her, she had simply felt that something was terribly wrong and had phoned the Elsinore drop zone where she learned of his death. She came home immediately, attended his funeral, and, I was to learn later, had helped Michael's family sort through his personal effects.

She was present when the copy of my will was discovered, naming Michael my primary heir. It was a shock to her since she had known nothing of my relationship with him. Michael died just before we were to make our relationship public. Nance knew me no better than I knew her, but suspected that Michael and I were serious about each other, as evidenced by my will. Probably out of curiosity more than anything else, she wanted to get to know me to see for herself if and why I had been the one with whom Michael was planning a future.

A few days after his funeral, I heard her voice on the phone.

"Hi, Bonnie? It's Nance. Nance Grutman."

My own voice stuck in my throat. I didn't know what she knew about Michael and me, and I didn't want to cause her any more pain by telling her. Losing a man through a breakup was one thing, but losing him through his death was something else. I knew, though, that I wouldn't lie if she asked me directly.

Clearing my throat, I took a deep breath. "Nance,

how are you?" I felt genuine concern for her. I still felt connected to everyone Michael had loved, including her. After all, we had something special in common. We knew what it was like to be loved by him. No one could identify with us more than we could with each other.

Her voice registered relief, perhaps because I sounded neither threatening nor patronizing. "Bonnie, I was in Michael's apartment when your will was found. I'm embarrassed to admit it, but I read it. I can't imagine you would leave everything to a man who, well...I guess I'm fishing for answers. Michael kept you a secret from me and evidently from a lot of others. You must have loved him deeply. I'm sorry."

I could tell she meant it. "Nance, I'm so sorry for you, too. I'm glad you were there to help Ib with his things. I just couldn't deal with it. I don't mind that you found my will. I just hope it didn't hurt you."

"To tell you the truth, I was shocked but also relieved. I know some of the other women he dated. When we broke up, I just had this feeling that it was a set-up. He prearranged a set of circumstances that he knew would encourage me to break up with him, instead of vice versa. I think he figured that wouldn't hurt me as much. I felt that it was intentional and wondered if he was going to marry one of those other women. It would have hurt worse to think of him as being alone or with someone less than he deserved. I would be glad to know that it was you he had chosen."

I couldn't bring myself to confirm that over the phone. In fact, it would be several months before I confirmed it to her at all. I wanted to see her for myself, to be certain that she would be okay with what I might tell her. I had never rejected Nance or been spiteful toward her as some of the other women at Elsinore had, but this might only mean to her that I was a lesser evil. I needed to see her in person before telling her about Michael and me. We talked for a while longer, sharing with each other parts of our separate histories with Michael. Finally we decided to continue our conversation in person a few days later.

When she arrived at my apartment, we looked into each other's eyes, and it seemed that no one on Earth could know more about what we were going through than we ourselves. We embraced and cried, feeling instantly like sisters. Cathartically, we relived our experiences with the man we both loved, and that day brought each of us a friendship that has survived the test of many years.

Nance had found something else in Michael's apartment that she suspected was connected to me. "Do these have any meaning for you?" she asked, as she handed me the risers from the parachute I had bought him.

I could not choke back the tears.

"I thought so," she said softly. "I realize now it was you he was honoring on the risers."

I thanked her as I fingered the silky, stenciled fabric marked B4M.

"This wasn't from the parachute that brought him down, was it?"

"No, that was another one."

As we talked, and day turned to dusk, I turned on the lamps in the living room. Within minutes, the lights flickered, ever so slightly, as if Michael were winking his approval of our friendship.

We visited each other often, our relationship growing stronger each time. One starry night as we sat on the patio outside her home in Perris, we talked about our pasts, and what course our lives might take in the future. There was a wonderful feeling of peace and comfort that night and the unmistakable feeling that Michael was present. I told her about my belief in reincarnation and some of the lives I felt I had lived before. In fact, during a recent meditation, I had seen how my interest in art had begun centuries ago in China.

I had seen myself as delicate with almond-shaped eyes, clear porcelain skin, a small, curved nose, but with a slightly irregular mouth, giving a sense of disharmony to an otherwise flawless face. I saw myself painting a large scroll stretched over a frame. When the paint was dry the scroll would be rolled up for easier transport. I lived within the walls of the Emperor's city and was distantly related to him, perhaps a cousin. My right to live within these walls amid opulent grandeur was not secured by my birthright, however, but by my value to the Emperor as an artist.

I painted serene landscapes, but hidden within the scenes were messages the Emperor used to communicate with his generals in the field. My country was at war and this was a reasonably secure way to transmit information.

There was sadness for me though, for the war seemed so futile. I loved my country and understood my people's fear of an enemy that could attack them and destroy their crops at any time. I also knew that the protection of the city's walls was mostly an illusion. They could be breached by a determined force and I knew it was only a matter of time before we, too, were overrun. I painted, painstakingly striving to become better, not just for art's sake, but to better serve my country and my people.

Then I told Nance about the psychic's message regarding my life with Michael during the civil war. I was fascinated but had never seen anything pertaining to it in my dreams or in meditation. I wondered from time to time who he and I had been, but perhaps I was not ready for this information.

Amazingly, Nance too, felt that she had lived before, and related, in great detail, the experience of drowning when the Titanic sank. She saw herself as an old woman taking the voyage with her husband whom she greatly loved. Because of her age and the necessity to separate from him if she was to try for a place in a lifeboat, she elected instead to die with him in their cabin. She told of how she felt, seeing the water bursting through the cabin as the ship went down.

She and her husband clung to each other without struggling, and, once underwater, she simply took in a deep breath. A feeling of peace came over her. There was no pain. Because of her own untroubled memory of dying by drowning, she was not disturbed about how Michael died, only by the fact that he had.

As our conversation turned from the distant past to the future, I told her that I was thinking about applying to an art school for more training. My art teacher was encouraging me to seek out more formal education. She had taught me all she could, and she felt that I should stretch myself at a good school. Nance thought I should do it, and the words she used to convey this to me could have come right out of Michael's mouth. Then it was my turn.

"I don't know what to do with my life," she said. "I don't want to go back to teaching or sewing parachutes for a living, yet I don't know what else I want."

Just then I felt the words in my head as I asked her, "What have you done in your life that made you the happiest?"

Without a moment's hesitation, she answered,

"I always loved college. I loved to learn. That was such a special time for me."

"Then maybe you should go back. Work toward a degree, or not. It doesn't matter. To be in the environment you've always loved may be just what you need now to get some breathing space to heal. And who knows, it could lead to something else for you."

The advice must have hit a chord, for she admitted that she had thought a long time ago about working for a Ph.D. in literature but had dismissed it as frivolous. But now it seemed like the right thing to do. We both knew that there would still be many dips and turns in our lives, but at least that night we found ourselves with a plan and goal.

A few months later, Nance was again in Indiana on a month-long exercise for the Army Reserve. On a pass one day, she attended a show of Civil War photographs taken by the famous photographer of that era, Mathew Brady. The exhibit was displayed in a local shopping mall and as she wandered among the photos she came across one that immediately stopped her. Before her was the face of a man known as General John Hunt Morgan of the Army of the Confederacy. It belonged to another place and time, but it was Michael's face that looked back at her.

There was more than a physical resemblance. General Morgan and Michael shared the same facial structure, hairline, and Van Dyke beard, but more than that, there was an uncannily familiar look in Morgan's eyes. If there was such a thing as "soul recognition," Nance was experiencing it as she gazed into the face of a man who had died over a hundred years ago.

There was often a quality in Michael's expression that made me feel like I was looking into a deep well of experience reflecting eons of both tragedy and joy. It was as though Michael had seen and experienced all the pain and suffering of the world and had somehow come through it with compassion and understanding. It was not that he was the only person to have experienced all that, but the degree to which it showed on his face and in his eyes was remarkable. Now, looking into the face of this other man who lived so long ago, Nance saw that same quality and depth of expression.

She wasted no time in finding out all she could about him. She discovered a book published in 1976 called *Morgan and His Dixie Cavaliers*, by William E. Metzler. She contacted the author and bought two copies. She sent me one, along with a copy of Morgan's photograph.

As I unwrapped the package, I found a note taped to the tissue paper around the book. "Does this remind you of anyone we know?" I unwrapped the photograph first and saw Michael's face over a confederate officer's uniform. The shock stopped my breath and weakened my knees, but the shocks were just beginning.

Inside the book was another photo of General Morgan. In this one he sported a cavalier's hat, with one side tacked up like a modern day "bush" hat, the only style of hat Michael had ever owned. I collapsed into a chair and began turning the pages, somehow knowing that I was a part of this history.

Chills went down my spine at the sight of the Morgan family home in Lexington, Kentucky. General Morgan's father had built it around 1813 and John had been born there. It was the manor house I'd seen in my meditation. The Georgian-style mansion was called Hopemont, and the most distinctive exterior feature was the elaborate fan-shaped windows above the front door.

I was disappointed, however, when I read about his marriage. His wife, Rebecca Hunt Morgan, seemed to be nothing like me, in temperament, physical likeness, or personality. It wasn't that I expected to see my face on top of someone else's body, but I had hoped to recognize something of me in her.

I wanted to be the wife of John Morgan, which would explain Dorothy's message about my marriage to Michael in a past life during the Civil War. I had identified with the Southern belle type of woman of that era, a survivor, like Scarlet O'Hara in *Gone with the Wind*. Her, I could relate to, not meek and frail

Rebecca Hunt.

But as I read on, I learned that Rebecca had died young. Morgan was bereft but within a few years married a woman with whom he fell deeply in love. Her name was Martha and was known as Mattie to her friends. She was described as a "Southern belle." As I turned the page and saw the picture of Martha, I was not only looking into my own eyes, but I realized that I had seen her in this lifetime. She was the one in the meditation I'd had years before ever knowing Michael, standing in front of a manor house with her daughter, in deepest grief. I identified completely with the woman in the photograph. How poignantly I had felt her grief during my meditation. It was a degree of pain I had not known in my own life then, but one I knew all too well now.

They were married only a few years when General Morgan was killed, not in battle, but by a young Union soldier who, on capturing him, choose to kill him instead of taking him prisoner.

It was clear to me now what Dorothy had meant when she'd said that my history had repeated itself. I lost him in that life as I lost him in this. How cruel it was to lose the same love in two lifetimes. Why had this had to happen? Tears of frustration blurred the words, but I continued.

Just before General Morgan's capture and subsequent death, his men learned that there was a Union regiment en route to where the general was bivouacked for the night. Only one had tried to save him, but he was too late. His men had felt that the general was invincible. He had in fact been captured and later exchanged for other prisoners of war on two previous occasions.

The witnesses' accounts of Michael's death immediately came to mind. They, too, did nothing to retrieve him from the lake until it was too late to save him, except for the one jumper who'd seen his reserve from the other side of the lake. He, too, arrived too late. In my dream, Michael's own account of his death corroborated this. They hadn't been paying attention.

Had Michael's death been preordained? Had the men in Morgan's regiment been reincarnated into the jumpers on Michael's fatal skydive so that they might be given a chance to save him this time? But again they failed to do so. I heard the words "free will" pop into my mind, reminding me of its impact on one's destiny. The universal design to make another choice may have existed, but if it had, the souls involved had the choice, singly or collectively, whether or not to act differently this time. They choose not to. I asked Michael if I was right in this assumption and was answered with the chill of confirmation.

As I read on about General Morgan, I marveled at the personal values and personality traits he shared with Michael. Morgan contributed to the war effort by delaying and disorganizing the enemy. He attacked their railroad and telegraph lines. Sometimes he would leave cryptic notes for the enemy, salting the Union army's frustration with humor. At every opportunity, though, he spared Union soldiers' lives, choosing to harass the Yankees rather than contribute to more carnage. Morgan did not play by the rules. The Union army hated and feared him because they couldn't understand him. He was so reviled by them that the young soldier who killed him thought himself to be a hero.

Michael, too, had an aversion to convention. Like Morgan, he had a finely tuned sense of humor, a huge appreciation for life, and was often misunderstood by his contemporaries.

Morgan had been captured twice and suffered greatly in a Yankee prisoner-of-war camp before being exchanged for officers held by the Confederate army. Michael had had nightmares that had centered around imprisonment or imposed confinement. He'd never been jailed in his life so I'd always thought it an odd fear. Now I knew that his spirit was remembering the torment from this past life.

Mattie had shown great courage and love for her husband. On several occasions she had ridden horseback inside territory held by the Union army in order to rendezvous with him. Their love had been born amid the havoc and chaos of those war years, and they could see each other only sporadically and often under dangerous conditions. She became pregnant with their first child and on return from one such rendezvous was herself captured by the Yankees and held for a time as a prisoner of war. She lost that baby in childbirth.

After her release and recovery, she again met with her husband and subsequently became pregnant with their daughter. This child was born after Morgan's death. I believed this was the daughter I saw in front of the manor house in my meditation.

I sat for a long time after finishing the book, grateful for Michael's efforts to bring it to me. The door to this other world was now open and as I relaxed my mind, I saw vignettes of our past life: dancing slippers darting from under hooped skirts, and petticoats sailing over a polished wood floor as dancers stamped out the rhythm of a southern reel. Pecan tarts dipped in honey. Candlelight reflected in the mirrored walls of a ballroom. And the eyes of the man who was to be, all too briefly, my husband. This I knew, was the night we met. A wave of sadness passed over me as I saw these scenes from the life I had lived a hundred years before, a life that foreshadowed so much to come.

I had asked myself so many times, "Why did Michael have to die?" Now possibly Michael himself had shown me the reason. I might never be able to convince anyone but myself, but I knew in my heart that his death, although preordained, could also have been prevented. Perhaps the purpose was to provide a new scenario for those inattentive soldiers of the past to redeem themselves. Or perhaps it had more to do with the personal lessons each of us was to learn from the event, including Michael. There were decisions at Elsinore that he, himself, could have made that might have saved his life.

He had always been fastidious about safety preparations preceding a jump. Yet, instead of a motorized boat launched prior to the jump, there was only an unattended rowboat beached on the shore. Michael would have noted this oversight and could have postponed the shoot. For whatever reason, he did not.

Michael may not spell out all the "ifs," "ands," and "whys" for me concerning his death, but he was giving me the information I needed and he'd gone to a lot of trouble to do that. The remainder would have to remain an enigma for the time being.

Marriage

16

Jeanne was getting married again. This would be her third marriage. To celebrate, I painted her a picture of a rustic mailbox nestled in tall grass and trees beside a country road. Painted on the side of the mailbox was her maiden name crossed out to reveal the last name of her first husband. This, too, was crossed out and below it was the last name of her second husband, also crossed out. With no more room for names, I hung a rider sign from the mailbox showing the name of her future husband, not crossed out. She loved it.

"Let's have a girls' night out, dinner and a movie," I suggested. "We can talk, eat, giggle, and gossip." Jeanne was game, especially since there would be few nights like this between us once the last set of "I do's" was pronounced.

In the darkened theater after the last scene of the movie, Jeanne heard me sniffling. I was relating deeply to the love story on the screen. My own love story was history. Unlike the film, this aspect of my life would not have a happy ending.

Jeanne placed her hand on mine, patting it gently. "Do you think you'll ever love again, Bonnie? I want you to be happy."

It had been almost two years since Michael's passing and in that time I had found a comfortable life for myself filled with a few good friends like Jeanne. My life wasn't all that I had wished for, but it was better than I could have imagined in the months immediately following Michael's death.

There was now an added perspective, an awakening to a spiritual dimension which now colored all aspects of my life. I still had my nightly visits to the other side, most of them shared with Michael. Jeanne knew some of this, but it was difficult for me to articulate much, even to myself. Her question, however, pertained to my waking, conscious world.

"I can't imagine that ever happening," I finally answered. "It's not that I've lost the ability to love. I've come to love a lot of people on a spiritual level. But even if I could see the possibility of loving someone else in a romantic relationship, I can't see myself ever marrying. The spiritual side of myself is something I would never hide, especially my connection to Michael, and I think that would be threatening to another man. I wouldn't want to duplicate what I had with Michael, but neither would I deny it to please someone else. Most men I've known would want to be *the* number one in a woman's life."

Jeanne nodded knowingly. "Yeah, I've had a hard time convincing each husband that he was better than the last."

***

On the other side, Michael and I were standing beside a shiny, brass bed in the middle of a magnificent meadow. A lovely woman walked up a knoll toward us, then stopped at its edge. Michael turned to me and said, "What we've had and always will have, B, remains between us; something that only we've shared. That will never be lost." He rested one hand on the brass headboard, intimating the physical passion we had known. Around us was nature in its most splendid setting, symbolizing the spiritual love that surrounded us.

He told me that I needn't be afraid that in loving another, it would take away from us. Love was not something to hoard. I should feel love and give it away. "The more cherished you are by others, the more cherished you are to me," he said.

Michael's eyes shone as I looked into his face and saw our history together, felt the various dimensions of love we had known for each other in all the lives we'd shared. Then I looked at the woman on the knoll. I knew of no history between us, yet I felt a similar bond with her. She focused on both of us and I felt myself return the love she radiated. The commonalty of spirit that connected us had nothing to do with past knowledge of each other. As I looked at her, she became neither female nor male but, rather, a spiritual light encompassing both energies. Spiritual love, I intuited, has *no gender.*

In an instant I was alone, no longer on the meadow but walking along a cobblestone street with gas-lit lampposts from another century. A group of people I didn't recognize greeted me with excited voices, as though they knew me well, telling me my wedding was about to take place. They hurried me, pulling me along with them to prepare me for the event. I felt like an amnesia victim, confused as to what these people were talking about, but I surrendered to them anyway.

We entered a large modern room with enormous picture windows, and waiting there for me were my mother and bridesmaids, also unknown to me. They were elated over my wedding. I said to my mother, "I don't have a wedding gown. I can't get married in my old one."

She produced a beautiful blue lace gown with flowing skirts and helped me into it. "Did anyone order flowers?" I asked. Instantly, boxes of long-stemmed, thornless, red-and-white-striped roses appeared.

"But who am I to marry?" I asked.

An usher then entered the room and handed me a wedding invitation   inscribed "Mr. and Mrs. Sid Gold request the honor of your company at the wedding of their daughter Bonnie to..." I saw only an empty space where the groom's name would go. But as I continued to look at it, the name "Michael" slowly appeared.

I awoke, puzzled. Did the wedding mean that

Michael and I would be married on the other side after my transition there? Perhaps he was showing me how, spiritually, we were already married. Yet the old-fashioned street lamps at the beginning of the dream and the modern room at the end, seemed to tell me I was moving from the past into the future. I was being given part of the puzzle, but the rest of it remained an enigma. Why, for example, was my mother the only person I recognized?

***

I was slowly slipping back into my own orbit again, no longer riding copilot to the spirit that had guided me through the past two years. I was taking back control of my life. The visits to the other side, the lessons learned there, and the knowledge that Michael's spirit still existed and was watching over me continued to give me strength and a sense of life's higher purpose. Inevitably, graduation day came.

Michael and I walked through the same meadow, hand in hand, as on my first visit to the other side. "It's time for you to go back, B. You can't come here like this anymore. It's time to get back to the living."

I felt the wisdom in his words, but also sadness. I had become dependent on my nightly visits and his support. I knew that I would continue to miss him on

Earth, but now it was time to continue on my own.

"When I make my transition here, will it be like the experience I had as a child?" I asked.

No, he told me. That experience was what I needed at that time. It taught me the connection of life to all other life, leaving me with a reverence for nature, people, and animals. I experienced spirituality in its purest form, unclothed by religion because that was not part of my consciousness. If I'd had an affinity for a particular religion, my experience would have been much different. My future experience, he added, will be colored by the addition of events in my life since then.

"Everyone receives what they need at the time of transition. Each experience is the truth for that person, at that time; that is, their perception of truth. But perception, and therefore truth, changes. You're different now and you will continue to change."

I thought of how I had changed since Michael's death. I had viewed myself, in large part, by how others saw me. I was fearful of losing Larry. I thought if I became voluptuous, he would want me more. So I had my breasts augmented. When I lost a breast, Larry saw me as devalued, and, as a result, I saw myself that way. I feared being viewed as a rejected, divorced woman and so I endured indifference and loneliness in my marriage. I feared Larry's wrath, so I kept my love for Michael secret.

I had lived much of my life in fear of something bad happening as a result of something I did or failed to do. But now I felt a kind of freedom. Life is so complex, I'd learned, that my futile efforts to control whatever happened were infantile. Of course my actions make a difference, everybody's does, but I cannot predict what the outcome will be, so why should I try to control it? The outcome is a consequence of a combination of events I can hardly perceive.

When I physically lost what I valued most in life — Michael — I was freed from fear of future loss. When I came to realize that I would never lose his spirit, I found I had gained that part of him that I would never have known existed prior to his death.

As a result, I gained a spiritual strength I could not have had without all the trauma, as well as the revelation, of the past two years. I never would have supposed that anything good could come from Michael's death. Yet, I felt enormously strong, tempered from the ordeal, and changed in a way that I knew in my very being would last far beyond my own death.

"What about my experiences over here, the lessons I've learned? Was that just for me and the other spirits I shared them with?"

He told me that I saw those "scenes" because I needed to see them that way in order to absorb them. He said that because my personality loves teaching, classes, and being a student, the metaphors and symbolism had personal meaning for me. Other people have other ways of learning. Their scenarios might be different, although many of the lessons could be the same. Even though there were others in my classes, they did not necessarily see or hear the same things I did.

"All this," he said, as he swept his hands in a circle, "is your metaphor for the information you received from your spirit. This information, and even more, has been given to you, but you would not remember it or be able to interpret it without the scenic detail, people, and conversation you experienced."

He was giving me his enormous grin now. "Go on, B, you've almost got it. Ask the question."

I, too, did a circular sweep of the land around us and asked, "What is this place? Is it another dimension in space and time, is it a dream? Where are we, really?"

"It's where you live. The real you. It's your real life. You didn't visit here, Bonnie. You live here, all the time, always have, always will." He laughed aloud, obviously happy to be my source of enlightenment. "It's the beginning, end, and intermission of life. It's everything you think it is and far more than the human mind can perceive. Earth, this other side, and other dimensions as well, all coexist together. Most people either don't know that or don't remember it. Why do you think you need sleep at night? It's not to rest the body. It's to give your spirit breathing space to work out the details of the Earth experience without the encumbrance of the body.

Dreams, he said, aren't random snatches of unrelated sights and sounds. That's just how people remember them. Everything is worked out here before it's reflected there. Science can prove the existence of the other side. The evidence is there if they'd acknowledge spiritual existence, but they don't recognize it. Yet there would be no science on earth if it wasn't here first.

"You were given a special gift, B. — the gift of remembering and interpreting. Your mind and heart were open to it. You were raised in this lifetime to be open to it because, before you were born, you agreed to accept it.

"The lessons and experiences over here won't end, nor will the guidance you'll receive or the love you feel. But it's time to focus on the plane of existence in which your goals and destiny can be fulfilled. Earth is where your consciousness belongs now."

His eyes reflected the universe, filling me with a rainbow of feelings, thoughts, and memories. My eyes filled with tears, and through their prism I saw a dozen Michaels fading before me as he said, "You won't remember seeing me much now, but I'm not far away, B. I'm just on the other side."

Epilogue

Over the next five to six years, my spiritual awareness led me to friendships with others who shared my values. Despite the closeness I felt to them, I never told anyone entirely about the incredible experiences I'd had on the other side. It seemed too personal at the time, and I was still processing it. I would speak of an episode when I felt it appropriate, but I was not ready to expose myself to public scrutiny.

I was not lonely, although I knew I was not living the life I would have had with Michael. I retained an inner peace and I appreciated both the beauty and the challenges life offers.

One evening in January 1989, I was coming out of an evening church service at the Church of Religious Science in Huntington Beach, California, when just outside the chapel doors, I saw a man looking directly at me. He was smiling brilliantly, as though he knew me. He was muscular and athletic. He had dancing blue eyes and short, sandy-brown hair. I could not turn away as I searched my memory for an indication of how I knew him. As if prearranged, he fell into step with me and we began to talk.

"Hi," he said. "My name is Michael."

We were married one year later, almost to the day we met. I had been wrong. There *was* someone out there who could understand and accept my relationship with my first Michael. In fact, my husband gives thanks to him. Because of him, I became the woman my husband fell in love with. Our life together has been spiced with many challenges but as my first Michael had promised, the relationship has been easy.

The wedding I saw from the other side finally made sense. The Michael I was marrying was Michael Cox. My mother was on the other side by that time; she had made her transition there two weeks before my wedding. There were one hundred human guests at our wedding, plus two very happy spirits.

It is never the end!

Bonnie Cox has undergone twenty-two surgeries in her lifetime, including three open-heart, three spinal fusions, and eleven breast surgeries as a result of a botched initial breast implantation.

Prior to her introduction to the "other side," she had occasional psychic experiences. As a teenager, she saw, superimposed on her father's face, the face of her grandmother at the moment of her death, three hours before the family was notified. This ability may be genetic. Her mother was awakened one night by her deceased father-in-law who informed her that she was pregnant with a son and asked her to name her son after him. At age thirteen, as recounted in the prologue to *The Lightbearer*, Bonnie had a near-death, out-of-body experience when her heart stopped for two minutes during spinal surgery.

Bonnie's short story, "I Love You", appears in *Chicken Soup for the Soul Cookbook*, by Jack Canfield, Mark Victor Hansen, and Diana von Welanetz Wentworth. She appeared on the television show, The Other Side, where she discussed her relationship with her guardian angel and deceased fiance, Michael Jenkins, and how her husband, Michael Cox, has been affected by his presence. She has been a guest speaker on the near-death experience at Golden West College.

She lives with her husband in Newport Beach, California.